# PINNACLE ON THE MOUND

# PINNACLE ON THE MOUND

## *Cy Young Award Winners Talk Baseball*

## **Doug Wedge**

ROWMAN & LITTLEFIELD
Lanham • Boulder • New York • London

Published by Rowman & Littlefield
An imprint of The Rowman & Littlefield Publishing Group, Inc.
4501 Forbes Boulevard, Suite 200, Lanham, Maryland 20706
www.rowman.com

6 Tinworth Street, London SE11 5AL

British Library Cataloguing in Publication Information Available

**Library of Congress Cataloging-in-Publication Data**

Names: Wedge, Doug, author.
Title: Pinnacle on the mound : Cy Young Award winners talk baseball / Doug Wedge.
Description: Lanham : Rowman & Littlefield, [2021] | Includes bibliographical references and index. | Summary: "In Pinnacle on the Mound, ten Cy Young Award-winning pitchers recognized as the very best at their craft share amusing anecdotes and valuable insight about their keys to success. From Jim Lonborg to Corey Kluber, their fascinating stories represent 50 years of baseball history"—Provided by publisher.
Identifiers: LCCN 2021017408 (print) | LCCN 2021017409 (ebook) | ISBN 9781538154816 (cloth) | ISBN 9781538154823 (epub)
Subjects: LCSH: Pitchers (Baseball)—Anecdotes. | Baseball—Anecdotes. | Cy Young Award.
Classification: LCC GV871 .W43 2021 (print) | LCC GV871 (ebook) | DDC 796.357/22—dc23
LC record available at https://lccn.loc.gov/2021017408
LC ebook record available at https://lccn.loc.gov/2021017409

# CONTENTS

# ACKNOWLEDGMENTS

I am grateful to the 10 Cy Young Award winners who agreed to share their time and perspective. Thank you to Jim Lonborg, Mike McCormick, Randy Jones, Ron Guidry, LaMarr Hoyt, Dennis Eckersley, Jack McDowell, Barry Zito, R. A. Dickey, and Corey Kluber. Josh Thole also agreed to an interview to discuss his experiences working with R. A. Dickey, and I appreciate his sharing his insight. Thank you to Sheri Rosenberg, Becky Biniek, Dierdre McCormick, Brandon Guidry, Jennifer Eckersley, Bo McKinnis, Kraig Williams, and Stephanie Khoury for coordinating these interviews. I owe Lyn Marshala a debt of gratitude for transcribing several of these interviews.

John Horne at the National Baseball Hall of Fame and Museum generously reviewed archives, retrieved photographs of the pitchers, and shared them for inclusion in the book. The library systems of Jefferson County (Alabama) and Oklahoma County (Oklahoma) were invaluable research resources. Thank you, all.

Thank you to Leigh Dudley, Charlie O'Brien, George Singleton, Steve Skinner, Willie Steele, and Justin Werner for reading early drafts of these chapters and offering suggestions and advice for improving them.

I appreciate the kind, patient, and talented team at Rowman & Littlefield who took a chance on this book and devoted their time and resources to ensure it could be shared with an audience. I am especially grateful for Christen Karniski for sharing ideas for strengthening the manuscript and for Erinn Slanina and Andrew Yoder for guiding me through the production process.

Thank you to the readers who pick up this book and spend your time with it.

Thank you to Shawn, Jack, Annie Sloan, Sophie, and Sadie for all that each of you do to make the world a better place.

# INTRODUCTION

Consider having an interest in a particular field and what an opportunity it would be to shadow someone who has achieved great success mastering that craft. The songwriter who can spend time with the seasoned musician and observe the musician's approach to composing music and lyrics and ask questions about some of the songs they have written. The apprentice carpenter who has built five tables being able to work alongside the master who has built 50, looking over the mentor's shoulder as the mentor shares lessons and tricks gleaned from experience. The sous chef working for and with a James Beard–winning chef and discovering new ways of pairing ingredients.

Undoubtedly, observing a master at work provides insights. By no means does it guarantee a replication of success, that the songwriter has even one song recorded much less becomes the next Bob Dylan or Paul McCartney. The carpenter may never build a table with the same degree of sturdiness or style as the master. But studying these masters and how they approach their craft can help and inform others. An idea or an approach that has worked effectively for one may work just as effectively for someone else. Or it may be an inspiration to build on that idea, modify it slightly, and expand it.

In this case, the study of masters centers on pitchers, specifically Cy Young Award winners. Established in 1956 by Major League Baseball commissioner Ford Frick, the Cy Young Award annually honors the best pitcher in the American and National Leagues (although originally and until 1967, only one pitcher could earn the award for both major leagues). Criteria for the award are not tied to specific statistics in that the pitcher with the most wins or the lowest earned run average (ERA) automatically wins the award. Voters use their discretion to determine the "best" or "most outstanding" pitcher in each league. Beginning with Jim Lonborg (1967 American League) and ending with Corey Kluber (2014 and '17 American League), this book chronologically profiles 10 pitchers recognized as the best or most outstanding at their position in a given year. Importantly, these profiles are based on in-depth interviews with each pitcher. These interviews provided an opportunity for the pitchers to reflect and share their perspectives about their Cy Young seasons, the highlights and challenges, the keys to success that made them effective. Combining these profiles presents snapshots of baseball history spanning 50 years while also exploring the common threads of what helped these masters achieve success, from conditioning to forming a trusted partnership with their catcher . . . and more. This book does not provide a recipe of guaranteed pitching success, but it offers a closer look at exceptional pitching and shares insights, stories, and opinions directly from 10 individuals who reached the height of their profession.

# I

# IMPOSSIBLE REALIZED: JIM LONBORG

## 1967 AMERICAN LEAGUE CY YOUNG AWARD

*I chatted with Jim Lonborg on a sunny Sunday morning. We met at his office where he practiced dentistry in Hanover, Massachusetts. He sipped orange juice as we sat in the quiet lobby that offered no indication that a Red Sox legend worked there. Simple chairs, end tables, a few magazines to skim while waiting for an annual checkup and cleaning. Hanging on the wall was a 2015 schedule of Red Sox games. That was it. Nothing about Lonborg's being Boston's first Cy Young Award winner, a key to the Sox' magical 1967 season when they improbably won the American League pennant, a pitcher who delivered some of the finest performances in World Series history. Dr. Lonborg recalled moments and instances from his award-winning season nearly 50 years prior with insight and detail, but he added that, unless prompted by questions about who were the toughest hitters he had faced or what was his most memorable experience on the Red Sox, he usually didn't think much about baseball. "I have such a busy life with my dental practice and my grandkids and my yard and our travel and life in general," he said. "I'm always moving forward. You don't see much baseball stuff around here."[1]*

On the final day of the 1967 regular season, fans stormed Fenway Park's field and carried pitcher Jim Lonborg in their arms, celebrating the Red Sox' 5–3 victory over the Minnesota Twins.[2] The win guaranteed the Red Sox at least a playoff game against the Detroit Tigers to determine the American League pennant winner. And, if the Tigers lost later that day, no playoff game would be necessary: The Red Sox would be American League champs.

While fans celebrated a pennant within grasp, perhaps they were also toasting a team that finished in ninth place the year before now on the verge of the World Series.

Maybe they were excited about who they were carrying, a man who had just won his 22nd game of the season by beating Dean Chance, the Minnesota Twins ace whom he faced four times previously that season and lost all four games.

Nearly 50 years later, the scene remains vivid to Lonborg.

"In the beginning, it was so much joy, so much happiness," he says. "At first, my teammates were there, and we all knew something very special had happened. And, then they saw the fans running out, and they decided to get the hell out of there. Hats were getting torn away and stuff, but, for some reason, I just stayed out there. All of a sudden,

Lonborg on the mound and delivering in Fenway Park. Courtesy of the National Baseball Hall of Fame and Museum, Cooperstown, N.Y.

we're just moving in this sea of humanity to the right-field corner, and then I realized I didn't want to be going that way. I really wanted to be going *that* way. And, the police officers, there's a very famous picture of me being escorted off the field by two police officers with my jersey all ripped off and this look of fear on my face," he says with a laugh. "What turned out to be very joyous at the beginning got to be just a little bit sketchy at the end."

The game was a comeback win for the Red Sox. Down 2–0 going into the bottom of the sixth and facing Chance, who was still throwing the ball well, Lonborg led off for Boston by bunting the first pitch down the third-base line. Twins third baseman Cesar Tovar bobbled the ball, and Lonborg reached first safely.

"Dalton Jones, the very next pitch, hits a single," Lonborg says. "Jerry Adair, the very next pitch, hits a single. Carl Yastrzemski, the very next pitch, four consecutive first-pitch singles, and now the game is tied 2–2. We go on to score five."

After the Sox' five-run sixth inning, Lonborg scattered a few hits, gave up a run, but pitched a complete-game win. And that's when Fenway Park erupted in ecstasy.

Once in the clubhouse, Lonborg and his teammates huddled around the radio and listened to the Tigers play the California Angels. When the Tigers' Dick McAuliffe grounded into a double play to end Detroit's season with a loss, the celebration continued.

The Red Sox were American League champs.


## KEYS TO SUCCESS

In 1967, his third major-league season, Lonborg blossomed as an elite pitcher. He led the league in wins, strikeouts (246), and games started (39). He says, "A lot of little things happened that made me what I became in '67."

One was developing a new pitch.

"In the winter of '66, the ballclub asked me to go down to winter ball and work on throwing a breaking ball when I was behind in the count," Lonborg says. "No matter how good your fastball is, if guys are looking for it, they're eventually going to hit it. So, they felt there was one more thing I could do to enhance my ability to be successful: that was to have

**Red Sox team photo of Jim Lonborg. Courtesy of the National Baseball Hall of Fame and Museum, Cooperstown, N.Y.**

confidence in throwing a breaking ball when I was behind in the count. So, it would take away the opportunity of the hitter to just sit on one pitch. So, I went to Venezuela, and I pitched for two months down there. Came home just before Christmas with a newfound confidence in the sinker. Nowadays, they call it a two-seam fastball. Back then, it was just a sinker."

Returning to the States with the sinker, Lonborg headed for the ski slopes—Heavenly Valley in California's Sierra Nevada. For two months, he skied Monday through Friday until it was time to report to spring training. He credits skiing with strengthening his core, lower back, and thighs, and he arrived in spring training in the best shape of his life.

At spring training, he worked with a new pitching coach, Sal Maglie. When Maglie pitched for the New York Giants in the 1950s, he earned the nickname Sal the Barber for his proclivity to pitch inside, the ball coming so close to hitters it gave them a shave. Maglie explained to Lonborg the importance of pitching inside and why it's effective. Maglie's lessons were a revelation to Lonborg.

"It's something I never thought about," Lonborg says. "With the way my ball moved, there were a lot of right-handed hitters that just never felt comfortable at the plate. Especially if I threw inside. And, now, Sal teaches me that the effectiveness of pitching inside is that eventually it makes the outside part of the plate just a little bit further away. If hitters are aware I'm coming inside, they're tentative."

To illustrate, Lonborg compares pitching inside to golf.

"If you have a ball that's a big fade—if you hit it, it goes to the right if you're a right-hander. If you hit that ball in the middle of the fairway, it's going to fade over to the right-side rough. But, if you start that fade more to the inside with a fastball, it's going to move twice as much. Now, effectively, that ball on the inside is really going to take off, and hitters are going to freeze. When the hitter sees it coming in, it's just going to trick him. He's going to try to get out of the way. So, [Maglie] taught me the art of pitching inside, just to get the advantage of getting more of the outside part of the plate. It turns into being a pretty intimidating part of your personality and pitching style."

Applying Maglie's lessons, Lonborg threw enough inside pitches that were so inside that they hit the batter. In fact, he led the league in 19 hit batters in 1967.

Topping off the adjustments coming into the season, Lonborg mastered the four-seam fastball, another tip from Maglie.

"Sal knew what my strengths were, and he also knew that my ball moved so much that, when I got 3–0 on a hitter, I didn't have a lot of guarantees that I could throw a straight fastball that wouldn't move out of the strike zone," Lonborg says. "So, Sal taught me a four-seam fast-ball. And, it proved to be just one more pitch in your arsenal that allowed you to throw a pitch for a strike and keep a hitter potentially as an out as opposed to a walk."

Going into the season, Lonborg was optimistic about his and the team's chances. Although the 1966 club finished ninth, 26 games be-hind first-place Baltimore, the Red Sox played well during the second half. With the adjustments he made in the offseason, Lonborg became a more complete pitcher. With these improvements, he envisioned suc-cess.

"I always like to set goals for myself," he says. "I guess it was from courses I had taken in business at school that stressed the importance of goals. I think I have it written down somewhere where I wanted to pitch 200 innings, keep my ERA under 3.50. Strike out more than I walked. Have fewer hits than innings pitched. And, then not look at that anymore. Put it in an envelope, put it away, and not even think about it because now it's in your head."

## THE IMPOSSIBLE DREAM TEAM

Using gruffness and sarcasm to motivate players, first-year manager Dick Williams led the Red Sox. Thirty-eight years old and only three seasons removed from playing in the big leagues himself, Williams had guided Boston's top farm team, the Toronto Maple Leafs, to winning records in 1965 and '66 to develop his managerial chops. One game against the California Angels when Lonborg pitched six no-hit innings exemplifies Williams and his combative style. With the game tied at 1 in the bottom of the ninth inning, two outs, and a baserunner on third, Lonborg bounced an 0–2 curveball. Catcher Russ Gibson thought the ball skirted behind him, so he turned to retrieve it. But Lonborg saw the ball was still in front of the plate. He also saw Angels baserunner Jay Johnstone racing toward home. Lonborg hustled to scoop the ball and tag Johnstone, but Lonborg missed the ball. Johnstone scored, and the Angels won, 2–1.

Lonborg trudged back to the dugout and sat on the bench, dejected. He could see the ball still on the field. He could also see Dick Williams leaning over the railing, looking out over the field.

Teammate Rico Petrocelli approached Lonborg. He slapped the side of Lonborg's leg and said, "Hell of a game, Lonnie."

"Thanks, Rico."

Overhearing the exchange, Williams shook his head. "Hell of a game, my ass. Take a look at the fucking score."

Williams's combativeness irritated or angered some players, including Lonborg, but Lonborg says it pushed them.

"I didn't really like a lot of things Dick did, but I went out there sometimes with the attitude that I was going to prove to him that I was better than he thought I was," Lonborg says. "I was always out there to win and to prove to him that I was a winner. [Williams's style] was just another fire that got turned on that cranked up the heat for you."

Indeed, that curveball was the last one Lonborg ever bounced with an 0–2 count and a runner on third.

"[Williams] was all about teaching lessons, and his statement was obviously pointed at that. Lesson learned."

The management style may have rubbed players the wrong way, but there's no arguing with the results. The team won 92 regular-season games.

"Dick inherited a team that was just getting ready to become a championship team," Lonborg says. "And, I think his sense of discipline channeled all of that into a good positive force."

Without question, the team jelled. "We all had a generally good feeling about our team, about everybody's performances with Tony [Conigliaro]. Mike Andrews. George Scott. And Yaz, of course. All the role players, the Jerry Adairs, the George Thomases, and the Jose Tartabulls all brought a very special personality to the team. There were a lot of interesting guys on the team. They weren't cookie cutter at all. But they all blended well because everybody had a kind of unique sense of humor. You know, the little pranks that kept the clubhouse alive with humor. And, then, the fact that we just started winning games. Winning close games. Everybody contributing, from the everyday player to the bench player. Fans started coming out to the ballpark."

While the team played well, things fell into place. As an example, Lonborg recalls a game against the White Sox.

"There was a ball in Chicago. Ken Berry was on third base, and Jose Tartabull was in right field, and Elston Howard was at home plate. And it was a medium fly ball to right field. It was the bottom of the ninth inning. And Jose made the greatest throw in his whole life. Elston Howard had to jump up and catch the ball and then come down and sweep out the fastest runner on the White Sox. Everything you saw, you think, 'I can't believe that just happened.' For little Jose to make the throw. For Elston to catch the ball. To come down and get the fastest guy on the team, and we end up winning the ballgame. It was things like that that would happen during the course of the summer."

While the team enjoyed success on the field, they enjoyed camaraderie and each other's company away from the ballpark.

"We used to go out together and have dinners together, and we'd go to different bars and have a great time."

Part of this group included the sportswriters who covered the Red Sox.

"They'd be in the bar after a ballgame, and we'd all come in and sit down with the writers. Talk with the writers. Everything was always off the record. They saw the game from a perspective that was a really neat perspective, and so you could get information from them with regard to things that happened on the field. It was a big, happy family. It was a really nice relationship because, as players, we respected them, and we also trusted them, that some of the shit that we did stayed in the clubhouse or stayed in the bar or stayed in the lobby. They were always so honorable like that, so it made for a wonderful relationship."

Another aspect making the atmosphere pleasant: owner Tom Yawkey.

"What a great owner. He would always come into the clubhouse way before the game started and put on his uni, and he'd go out and play catch and pepper with the clubhouse guys, and he'd talk to whoever came into the clubhouse early. Just come up and sit down on the bench or down at the seat next to your locker and chat with you. If you were down, say you had a bad game the night before, he'd come down and ask you how you were feeling and kind of impart all the good things that happened in the game and not so much the bad things. Just to let you know he had your back."

As soon as the press arrived, Yawkey was gone.

"He really enjoyed his private time with his boys down there," Lonborg says. "He spared no expense. Even in the minors, we had great equipment. It was important to him to treat everyone at a high level."

Part of the Red Sox' and Lonborg's success in 1967 is attributable to a good defense. George Scott won a Gold Glove at first base, and Carl Yastrzemski earned one in the outfield. For a groundball pitcher like Lonborg, a solid defense was critical.

"I could remember my rookie year. We had Frank Malzone at third and Eddie Bressoud at short, Felix Mantilla at second, and Lee Thomas as first, and there would be times when [manager] Billy Herman would come out, and I had just given up five or six hits, ground balls that ordinarily would have been caught, and these guys couldn't get to them."

Herman would look at his young pitcher and say, "Jim, it's not your fault. These guys are a couple of steps slower than they were a few years ago. Just hang in there. Keep throwing that stuff. You're throwing great. Just hang in there."

The '67 Red Sox infused young defensive talent with Scott at first in his second big-league season, 23-year-old rookie Mike Andrews at second, 24-year-old Rico Petrocelli at shortstop, and second-year player Joe Foy covering third. The trend of fresh faces continued in the outfield of Yastrzemski, the elder statesman of the team at 27 and with six years of service time under his belt, and two 22-year-olds, rookie Reggie Smith in center and Tony Conigliaro in right.

"We had a really good defensive ballclub, so it gave me confidence to just go ahead and pound the strike zone and let them take care of the rest," Lonborg says.

Yastrzemski won the Triple Crown and MVP honors, providing significant offensive support with 189 hits, 44 home runs, 121 RBIs, and a .326 batting average.

"He was the first professional athlete that I knew of that hired a physical trainer, Gene Birdy out of the Colonial Gym up in North Shore, to train all year round," Lonborg says. "So, he too came into spring training in great shape. Prior to that, guys would, at the end of the season, they'd take their shoes, their glove, their jock, put it in a box, put the box in a closet, and close the door. And then walk away. And they'd come back in February, open up the closet door, pull out the box, and then go to spring training. They did nothing."

Yastrzemski was a contrast, and the consistent training produced results.

"Carl was able to stay healthy all year. He did everything possible with a bat, but he also made great strides as a defensive player in the outfield. Running catches, taking the ball off the wall, throwing guys out. I mean, he was what they call a five-tool player. Well, maybe a four and a half because his running could be exotic at times."

Although things were clicking well for the Red Sox and Lonborg, both dealt with challenges. In Detroit in July, the weather was so hot and humid that Lonborg lost 11 pounds during the game and suffered dizzy spells.

"This was before Gatorade was out yet," he says. "It was before people knew the importance of hydration. They would say if you drank too much water you'll get cramps. You weren't supposed to go swimming because it loosened up your muscles, and you weren't supposed to lift weights because it tightened up your muscles. There were all these bits of misinformation that were out there, so yeah. I had a high metabolism. I did lose 11, 12 pounds that game. My forearm, I'd throw a curveball, and my forearm would cramp up. I'd have to go back there, stretching it. But I had kind of a whippy action with my arm. I think I got in five or six jams. I think I left 11 or 12 men on base but just kept getting out of jams. And, that was a Sunday afternoon, and that's why I couldn't pitch in the All-Star Game. Because I think I had thrown about 120 pitches that game."

One severe setback was the beaning of right fielder Tony Conigliaro on August 18. Taking a fastball to the temple, Conigliaro missed the rest of the season and the next before returning to the Sox in 1969 and earning Major League Baseball's Hutch Award in 1970 for his fighting spirit and competitive drive.

"It was the worst sound I ever heard in my life when the ball hit him because it didn't hit and glance off somewhere. It just hit and fell. Just straight down, and he wasn't moving," Lonborg says.

Prior to the injury, Conigliaro was a catalyst for the team. Through 95 games, the All-Star already had 20 home runs and 67 RBIs.

"Tony was having a great year," Lonborg says. "And, he was, of all the clutch hitters on the team, I think a lot of the players would have said if there was somebody that you wanted to come up in an important situation where you wanted a run driven in or a base hit, they would want Tony at the plate because he was such an aggressive and good hitter at that point in his career. Not to take anything away from Yaz, but Tony was fearless up there, and that's one of the things that got him in harm's way. Because he waited until the last minute to launch a pitch. And, he stood right on top of the plate. So, anything that was going to come inside had the potential of hurting him."

Which is what happened when the Angels' Jack Hamilton's inside pitch got away from him.

"It got him right there on the orbit," Lonborg says with a grimace. "It was a shame. His career had no limits. But, you know, it was miraculous he ever came back and did so well. He was just the greatest kid in the world. Wasn't a troublemaker. Wasn't a carouser. He loved women. We used to chase the same girls around town." Lonborg chuckles. "He really was just a good, down-to-earth, fun-loving guy who loved to play baseball."

In addition to losing a core player, the Red Sox also juggled satisfying military obligations during the season. The team arranged for Rico Petrocelli, Dalton Jones, and Lonborg to join the army under the Six and Six program: six months of active duty followed by six years in the reserves. After the 1965 season, the three completed most of their six-month active service obligation. But, while Lonborg was rolling on the mound, he had some interruptions when he had to leave the Red Sox and spend two weeks at his army base in Georgia to attend to his military duties. When this happened, the team contacted Lonborg's commanding officer and asked if Lonborg could continue to make his starts.

"Rico and Dalton weren't able to be a part of that because it was crazy to fly them in just for one game."

But the army made it work for Lonborg, allowing him to leave camp midday on days he was scheduled to pitch. The team sent a plane and retrieved him to pitch that night's game.

"All you have to guarantee me," the commanding officer said, "is that he gets here by reveille in the morning."

The team was willing to uphold that bargain. Lonborg says the situation was odd, but he adjusted.

"You know, you're in good shape. You're on a roll. There were plenty of things that we could do at the summer camp to play catch and run and work out, similar to what you would do if you were with the ballclub."

## ROUTINE

Lonborg dominated in 1967. On April 28, he shut out the Kansas City A's and struck out 13. He took a no-hitter into the eighth inning against the Cleveland Indians. Twice, he struck out the side.

With the success and the inside pitching, Lonborg developed an intimidating persona.

"If you were, say, gifted like I was or lucky enough to have that and you had an intimidating style about you and you felt good about yourself all the time, it's a lot easier to walk out on the mound and know that you are better than anybody that comes to the plate," he says.

"Intimidating," yet Lonborg describes himself as a quiet, reserved guy in the clubhouse who enjoyed reading an interesting book as a way to pass the time. On road trips, he enjoyed visiting museums and local historical sites. But he prepared for games by listening to Sal Maglie share an advance scouting report on what the other team's hitters were hitting well and what they didn't like to hit. "It wasn't nearly as precise as it is now with all the IT these guys get. It must be dumbfounding for pitchers today to have all this information. We kept things very simple."

On days he pitched, Lonborg liked to eat a good breakfast and go see a movie that afternoon. "Just because it allows you to clear your mind of all the nonsense."

Once he arrived at the park, he met with his catcher to discuss how they would approach hitters.

"You would have a conversation with the catcher before you started the game. And, you'd go over the lineup, pretty much about how you wanted to get these guys out. You know, whether or not they were hitting hot, you still had to take your positive power thoughts and run it at hitters until they proved to you that wasn't going to work, and then you would switch whatever that game plan was."

In 1967, Lonborg worked with multiple catchers: Mike Ryan, Bob Tillman, Russ Gibson, and Elston Howard.

"That summer, I had such good stuff, it didn't make a big difference who was going to catch me, but I will admit that life became a little simpler when Elston got behind the plate," Lonborg says. "Not that Mike or Russ weren't highly competent catchers. There was just that edge of experience that Elston had that was special."

With that experience, Howard was an excellent game-caller.

"I was always of the opinion and found that I worked best when the catcher was calling 95 percent of the game. Because all I wanted to be able to do was to get the sign and then mechanically throw the pitch. I didn't want to have to spend a lot of time debating whether or not that was the right call. I just wanted to react to the signal. And I learned that from Elston Howard when he came over to us in '67 later in the summer. He just made my life so easy as a catcher—it just allowed me to become a mechanical machine and not have to become a real thinking and mechanical machine."

As a young single man in Boston in 1967, Lonborg enjoyed a good time. But he always had a good night's sleep before he pitched. He changed this approach to getting two good nights of rest before game days after a conversation with Sandy Koufax during the World Series in 1967.

"[Koufax] made the analogy about when you pull an all-nighter in college studying and stuff," Lonborg says. "You generally can go take that test and feel pretty good for the rest of the day, but then it's two days after when, all of a sudden, you hit this wall. And it made all the sense in the world. It changed my philosophy on how much rest my team deserved from me."

Later in his career, when pitching with the Philadelphia Phillies, Lonborg meditated before games. "You come from home. You've got five kids and all kinds of stuff going on. You need to just clear all that out of your head and meditate."

Lonborg used that emphasis on the here and now to deal with any subpar performances with Boston. "Whatever's happening today is the most important thing. I never would look back at all. It wasn't that I didn't remember. It's just that I chose to go ahead."

Lonborg relied on his familiarity with his mechanics to make physical adjustments. "I had a reproducible windup. Every pitcher, they have checkpoints. If you start seeing a little trend with balls going a certain direction, you make the adjustments to get you back to that original healthy checkpoint or that healthy motion. A lot of times, your heel may be coming down a little bit instead of being flat footed. And, so, you change where your landing spot was. You could see out in front of the mound. You could see where maybe you were getting a little too open, so you close it up a little bit."

On days he didn't pitch, Lonborg ran. He says part of his 1967 success was due to his strong legs. He also worked on his arm and threw some on his off days. This was by design.

"The action on your sinker would be better if your arm was a little bit tired. The faster a sinker goes through the air, the less the ability of the ball is to sink. So, if I threw 94, 95 miles an hour, the ball's going to be a little bit straighter. But, if I'm throwing 90 or 88, when that ball comes through the air at less velocity, the ability of that sink action on the pitch is going to be higher."

Lonborg also enjoyed pitching at his home field. Although Fenway has small dimensions with the Green Monster only 310 to 315 feet away from home plate, his first Red Sox pitching coach, Mace Brown, told him not to worry.

"This wall is going to help you as much as it's going to hurt you. So, don't think of it as a bad place to pitch," Brown said. "There's going to be a lot of balls hit off of you here that would have been home runs in other stadiums."

At Fenway, the grounds crew helped pitchers by leaving the infield grass a touch high, enough to slow ground balls. This was until Red Sox hitters complained about the grass slowing down their ground balls too much. The compromise: cutting the grass lower but dampening the grass immediately around home plate.

## WORLD SERIES

Although Lonborg savored the triumph of pitching the Red Sox to an American League pennant, there was more baseball to play—the October classic against the St. Louis Cardinals.

"We were underdogs, and I think we were just so happy that we had won the pennant that being in the World Series was just an afterthought because we didn't give ourselves much of a chance. . . . But we knew we were a good ballclub, and we knew we could go out and play pretty well. The Cardinals team was just an immense power."

Indeed. The Cardinals roster included four future Hall of Famers, and the talented team won 101 games in 1967. Unlike Boston, which scrapped and clawed until the final day of the season to clinch the pennant, the Cardinals won the National League by a comfortable 10

½-game margin over the second-place Giants and cruised into the Series.

Still. The Red Sox had made it this far. They had a chance. They could win it all, and, providing himself a tangible reminder of this chance, Lonborg wrote "$10,000" in his glove before the Series started.

"We were discussing incentives and stuff like that, and we knew that, if we won the World Series, our share would be $10,000. So, I wrote it in my glove so I would look at it every time I threw a pitch."

In the first game, the Red Sox narrowly lost to Cardinals ace Bob Gibson, 2–1.

"It was kind of an eye opener that, wow, we can play with these guys," Lonborg says.

That message was amplified when, in Game Two, Lonborg took the mound. He had his normal four days of rest, and, as he warmed up, he felt good physically. He read the scouting reports, and one of his goals was to keep fleet leadoff hitter Lou Brock off the bases. So, Lonborg began the game by relying on the strategy that had worked so well for him throughout 1967: He pitched inside to Brock and backed him off the plate.

"The first pitch of the game was a high inside fastball to him that knocked him down. That was just kind of like something I did a lot that season, just as a little punctuation mark," Lonborg says. "This is me pitching out here now, and I just want you to know that this is my territory in there."

As he settled into the game at Fenway Park that afternoon, Lonborg realized he had good action on his sinker. He had sharp focus. The combination of feeling good mentally and physically meant that everything was working for him. He was in the zone.

"Mentally, I was totally focused, and it was one of the best days I had where you have not only physical but mental working together where you can pretty much slice up the plate the whole night long. Which is what I did. It's like when Larry Bird gets that feeling of give me the ball because it's going to go in. Or [Joe] Montana can have one of those perfect games where physical and mental come together and create just a great effect on the field, and that's where I was that day. Everything was working in sync."

In this optimal performance zone, Lonborg retired the first 19 Cardinals he faced before walking Curt Flood in the top of the seventh.

While Lonborg handled pitching duties, the Red Sox took the lead behind Yastrzemski's solo home run in the fourth and Petrocelli's sacrifice fly in the sixth for a 2–0 score. In the bottom of the seventh, Yaz launched a three-run home run to push the lead to 5–0. And, going into the eighth inning, Lonborg hadn't allowed a hit. Four outs away from joining Don Larsen as the only pitchers to throw no-hitters in the World Series, Lonborg gave up a double to Julian Javier to end the no-hit bid. Lonborg soldiered on, though, retiring all remaining Cardinal hitters to seal a *one-hit* shutout. Placing Lonborg's performance in perspective: At the time, it was only the fourth one-hitter in World Series history. And the Red Sox were now tied with the mighty Cardinals at one game apiece.

Lonborg's next turn in the rotation was against Steve Carlton in St. Louis for Game Five. Although all starts in the World Series are critical, this one was especially crucial for Lonborg and Boston as they trailed the Cardinals one game to three. If the Red Sox won, they'd keep playing. If they lost, they'd go home.

"We were at the end of our rope. You had to make sure that there was nothing interfering with your thought process when you went out there because it was the most important game of the year."

Going into Game Five, Lonborg felt a little tired, but he was content with this. "Being tired is better than being really strong," he says. "Again, I was able to carry the same quality of stuff that I had in Game Two to Game Five. It doesn't happen that often you can physically go out and re-create pitches and location of pitches and keep hitters off stride. I think my control was just phenomenal from Game Two to Game Five, which always makes pitching a little bit easier when you throw the ball. Ended up getting a few runs to work with, and then got a few more late in the game, which made life easier because that ballclub could explode at any moment. And, for some reason, I, again, had that physical and mental moment going."

Again, Lonborg threw a complete game. This time, he surrendered only three hits and one run, a solo home run to Roger Maris in the ninth inning, and the Red Sox won 3–1 to survive and Lonborg earned his second World Series win.

The Sox went on to win Game Six, placing them one win away from bringing a World Series championship to Boston. With two days' rest, Lonborg took the mound at Fenway and faced Bob Gibson.

"I was praying that we score early off of Gibson," Lonborg says. "I had pitched on two days' rest two or three times during the course of the summer. You can't overthrow because you're tired, but, if you can get a few runs to work with early, it gives you a little bit more license to come after guys. And the knowledge was in those days, if you didn't get Gibson early, you weren't going to get him at all because it took him a while to kind of get cranked up. They ended up scoring a few runs early. I think when Dal Maxvill hit a triple off me off the center-field wall in Fenway, I knew I was in trouble because he was just a little skinny guy, and, for him to hit a triple, I said, 'Oh, shit.' But you just keep plugging."

Lonborg pitched six innings that afternoon, but Gibson threw a complete game and held Boston to just three hits. The Cardinals won the game and the Series, but Lonborg says the team made a statement with its performance.

"We proved a lot to ourselves and to the people around the country that we weren't just this funky little team that was in ninth place last year and won on the last day of the season. We're actually a very good baseball team."

Owner Tom Yawkey was so pleased with Lonborg's 1967 season that negotiating a new contract for 1968 lasted approximately 60 seconds.

"[General manager Dick] O'Connell called me into his office, postseason, and said, 'You had a really great year last year.'"

Lonborg nodded, thinking he earned $18,000 in 1967.

O'Connell continued. "Mr. Yawkey would like to reward you for your efforts."

O'Connell then presented Lonborg with a $50,000 contract for 1968.

"I thought it was very fair," Lonborg says. "When he offered me 50, I said, 'I think that's a great number.' They had a great year at the gate, and Mr. Yawkey was the most generous of the owners, and he wanted to spend money. He always thought it was important to put it back into the scouting system, go out and sign players."

## ACL

Just as Lonborg was at the peak, winning the Cy Young Award and being on a pennant-winning team, he suffered a devastating knee injury.

"I was back in Heavenly Valley, doing what I had done the year before with regard to conditioning and trying to stay in shape. It had been quite successful for me in '66, and I just couldn't see any reason why not to continue it. But I ended up skiing on a day I shouldn't have been skiing. The conditions were pretty tough, and I tore the ACL and the MCL in my left leg."

Lonborg skied to the bottom of the mountain and warmed up with a couple of hot toddies, hoping the injury wasn't severe. But when he stood from the barstool, his leg crumpled.

Lonborg met with a local doctor who examined the knee then asked, "What do you do for a living?"

"I'm a professional ballplayer."

"Well, I suggest you get this taken out because your knee is pretty much shot right now."

Lonborg then contacted the San Francisco Giants' team physician who, after seeing Lonborg, reiterated the message. He suggested Lonborg travel to Boston immediately for surgery.

Lonborg obliged and was in a cast for 13 weeks. Once he was out of the cast, the compromised knee had a ripple effect, impacting his shoulder. And, with the Red Sox, the injury never allowed Lonborg to regain his elite form. In 1971, the team traded him to Milwaukee.

"I was pretty pissed off because I wanted to stay in Boston. My wife and I had just gotten married, so I was angry that summer and wanted to prove to everybody that I was better than they thought I was."

To that end, Lonborg worked with Brewers pitching coach Wes Stock, who helped reshape Lonborg's outlook to pitching.

"He was incredibly helpful to me in how to put myself into a position to win more often. And, seasonwise, I had the most consistent year ever. I had like 25 or 26 games where I gave up three runs or less. So, I was very, very happy about that experience."

The next year, Lonborg was dealt to the Phillies. Lonborg achieved success, winning 17 games in 1974 and 18 in 1976, but he was a different pitcher.

"I was starting to transition from a hard sinker, blow-guys-away kind of pitcher to more of a finesse and control style. [Catcher Bob Boone] was able to help me start to get pitches on the outside corner just by, if you could establish the fact that you can make that pitch time after time like Greg Maddux. Just ping at the black."

In 1979, Lonborg began a new chapter. He entered Tufts University's dentistry program. After graduation, he established a practice outside of Boston. In 2015, now 73, Lonborg continues to care for his patients with baseball a small part of his present. He catches an occasional game at Fenway, and, while tending to his gardening chores on the four acres surrounding his home, he will tune in and listen to a Red Sox game on the radio. He also enjoys traveling and skiing and spending time with his 11 grandchildren. That doesn't leave a lot of time to remember his athletic accomplishments of nearly 50 years ago. But he continues to enjoy the game.

"I love the challenge of the pitcher against the hitter," Lonborg says. "I love the athleticism of the outfielders and the infielders. I love the challenges of the game, the thinking part of it. The casualness of it in the sense that it doesn't have a time frame to it, so it's a great way to spend a day sometimes."

# 2

# TURNING IT OVER—A NEW PITCH, NEW SUCCESS: MIKE MCCORMICK

## 1967 NATIONAL LEAGUE CY YOUNG AWARD

*Mike McCormick participated in a lot of baseball history. He made his major-league debut in Shibe Park, a field that opened in 1909, and his first home field was the Polo Grounds. He pitched 16 seasons in the big leagues, and, at a coffee shop in Cornelius, North Carolina, in 2014, he reflected on his baseball experiences, from early instruction from his father, to being in the big leagues just months after his high school graduation, to becoming one of the better left-handed pitchers in the league, to reinventing himself after a shoulder injury. Along the way, he worked with several different managers, and he observed qualities of good and not-so-good managers.*

Alvin Dark (Giants): *"Dark's strength was baseball knowledge. He was always a step ahead. He was thinking. He wasn't waiting for something to happen."*[1]

Gil Hodges (Senators): *"Gil Hodges was a good manager except he was a real stickler for rules. When he said be there in uniform and on the field at five, you better be there in uniform and on the field at five. Because he would be sitting right on the top step of the dugout, seeing who wasn't. And, he was just that way. Discipline was his lifestyle."*

Ralph Houk (Yankees): *"Houk was a good manager because he knew how to keep the guys that didn't play happy. [He would] pat them on the back. Tell them, 'I may need you today. Be ready for me.' And, then play you once in a while. But constantly tell you how important you were in your role, knowing that you may never play."*

*The less effective? Those who inflated their accomplishments as players. One manager in particular stood out to McCormick.*

*"He was just one of those guys who would walk around with his World Series ring and this and that. He was third string at best and never played, but you'd think he was in the Hall of Fame to hear him tell the story. 'I caught so-and-so,' and 'I did this.' And, you think, 'Come on. Numbers don't lie.'"*

*Indeed. In 1967 when he won the Cy Young Award, McCormick led the National League in wins with 22.*

If you had asked Mike McCormick during spring training of 1967 who would win that season's Cy Young Award, he wouldn't have named himself.

"I come back to San Francisco in '67, and my goal is to be a long reliever," McCormick says. "Spot starter. Occasionally come in and get an out. The story of a journeyman pitcher."

The likelihood of McCormick being named the National League's best pitcher was improbable. He had transitioned from a 17-year-old bonus baby heralded as the next Warren Spahn, to an All-Star, to an injured pitcher relegated to the minor leagues, to a student learning a new pitch to resurrect his career.

But McCormick achieved success in 1967 one start at a time. Literally.

"I pitched because Bobby Bolin or Gaylord Perry was hurt and missed a start. And I went nine innings. Which warranted another start. And, 11 starts later, I was still starting."

Specifically, on June 19, McCormick's record was five wins and three losses.[2] He had made nine starts and four relief appearances. Then he pitched a complete-game win against the Reds and started a seven-game winning streak, which included a 10-inning shutout of the Dodgers (beating Claude Osteen, who likewise pitched into the 10th inning). By the All-Star break, his record had shot to 11 wins and three losses. Three of the wins were shutouts.

Most were surprised by McCormick's success, including the manager of the National League All-Star team, Walter Alston.

"He sent me a letter apologizing for not including me on the All-Star team," McCormick says. "I ran into him a few weeks later and said he didn't need to apologize. I said I know the circumstance. I understand. It all happened so quick. I'm as surprised as anybody."

## A NEW, DECEPTIVE PITCH

During his sensational 1967 season, McCormick relied heavily on the screwball, the pitch he learned while playing for the Washington Senators in 1965 and '66, 10 years into his major-league career. The screwball is similar to a forkball or a split-finger fastball, an off-speed pitch that drops. "It's a lot of strikeouts on balls that bounce in front of home plate," McCormick says.

He included the pitch in his repertoire after Senators bullpen coach George Susce suggested McCormick throw more off-speed pitches. McCormick was receptive, but he told Susce he wasn't pleased with his changeup as a viable off-speed pitch.

"Do you want to throw the screwball?" Susce asked.

McCormick agreed to try it.

"I used to have that natural turn a little bit. My ball would tail," McCormick says, referring to his release point. Susce instructed him to build on and exaggerate that turning motion. Instead of releasing the ball straight ahead toward the catcher, the lefty McCormick needed to snap his wrist to the outside (to his left).

To develop the pitch, Susce and McCormick played catch in the outfield before games with McCormick throwing screwball after screwball.

"Turn it over," Susce encouraged. "Turn it over."

Initially, the results were uneven. The first year he threw the pitch, McCormick recalls many wild pitches bouncing in front of the plate. But he persisted. He used a grip similar to the circle changeup—sliding his index finger from the seams to the side of the ball, forming a circle with the thumb. The hand looks like it's making an "OK" sign. He discovered that the higher he placed his thumb, the slower the ball traveled. The slower its speed, the more it moved.

"You fool them with your arm," McCormick says. "You don't fool them with the ball. They're fooled initially by the speed of your arm.

And then here comes the ball. I'd bounce some, but so what? Get a catcher who can catch it."

Hitters *were* fooled with his newfound pitch, evidenced by McCormick striking out the side on June 4, 1967, against the Mets (the fifth inning) and repeating this feat on August 19 (the second inning against the Reds). With the success, he used the pitch more and more. In fact, he threw the pitch so often that his left arm has a permanent crook. "I can straighten my right arm out," he says, extending his arms. "Not my left."

## LOOKING BACK

Remembering his Cy Young season nearly 50 years ago, McCormick's home park and teammates come to mind.

Home was Candlestick Park. Built in 1958 and '59 and located on the western shore of the San Francisco Bay, games were often played in windy, damp, foggy, and chilly conditions, especially at night. Nonetheless, McCormick liked Candlestick.

"It was cool. You could have some real hot road trips where you're exhausted. I used to sweat a lot, and you didn't do that at Candlestick. In fact, you'd put a turtleneck shirt on. I had probably my best luck at Candlestick."

The records prove McCormick's point. While he won 11 games at home and 11 on the road, he threw five shutouts in 1967. Four were at Candlestick. His ERA was lower at home (2.77) compared to the road (2.92). He threw fewer innings at Candlestick (126 2/3) than on the road (135 2/3) but struck out more at home (79) than away (71).

Although McCormick liked how Candlestick's wind kept things cool, he acknowledges its unpredictability.

"It could be irritating because the wind never blew the same way twice during the game. You start the game, and it would be blowing from your left side, and you get to the fourth inning, it would be blowing in your face. And, in the later innings, it's blowing from third base."

While the wind was inconsistent, one steady factor was teammate Willie Mays, who had been one of McCormick's original teammates when he joined the club in 1956 as a teenager.

"The thing I liked about him was he always played when I pitched," McCormick says. "Willie didn't play day games after night games, especially later in his career, but he always did when I pitched. I don't know why. I never really asked him why. But, my opinion is Willie liked me. And, number two, I threw strikes. There was nothing worse than somebody who didn't throw strikes, and you're having to stand in the outfield all the time. You know, left foot, right foot. So, he knew I was going to throw strikes, and, if I had it, it was going to be a quick game."

By the end of the season, McCormick led the National League in wins. He credits things falling into place as the reason for his success.

"If I needed somebody to make a double play, and it was a routine double-play ball, they nailed it. It's just the routine things. If I needed a ball caught, they caught it. It wasn't a lot of luck. But I think that's the difference between good and mediocre or average: They just made the plays."

Throughout the season, McCormick kept in shape by running. Although postbaseball he ran two marathons ("My pitching coaches would have a heart attack if you told them that I've run two marathons"), he did not like running.

"None of the guys could really tell you they liked it," he says. "They couldn't tell you why they didn't like it. I think their feeling was, if you were a regular and you were pitching, you had to stay in pretty good shape just to do that. So, your pitching kept you in shape. If you weren't playing, then you had to do other things to keep in shape. That's when running became important. Because, the first that goes when you're pitching is your legs. If a pitcher's wild, it's not because of their arms. It's because their legs are getting tired. Can't lift it as high and stretch it as far."

After working with George Susce in Washington, McCormick was used to lots of running.

"He would run us from foul line to foul line. Most guys would run you from right center to left center, half the distance. Well, if you do half the distance over a period of a year, when the weather gets hot, you're just not in as good of shape."

Although McCormick was named the National League's best pitcher, he wasn't invincible. McCormick remembers Billy Williams and Vada Pinson as hitting him well (that season, Williams hit .308 against McCormick with two home runs, while Pinson maintained a .545 batting average against McCormick with three home runs). "It's surprising, though. I'm a lefty, and no right-handed hitter really owned me."

McCormick ended the season with a complete-game 2–1 win over Jim Bunning and the Philadelphia Phillies.

"I didn't have to pitch. We weren't going to go anywhere [note: The 1967 San Francisco Giants finished in second place, 10 1/2 games behind the St. Louis Cardinals]. I said, 'I've gone this far. Let me go one more game.' So, I did."


## BONUS BABY

Eleven years before winning the Cy Young Award, Mike McCormick threw his first pitch in the major leagues. He was 17. Slightly more than three months had passed since his high school graduation, yet he toed the rubber at Connie Mack Stadium (formerly Shibe Park) on September 3, 1956, and faced Stan Lopata leading off the bottom of the eighth inning.

"It was Labor Day. So, it was a good crowd. Not because the Phillies were doing anything. They were worse than the Giants. But it was a good holiday crowd, and it was a day game."

McCormick coaxed Lopata to hit a ground ball to second base for the first out.

He faced two more batters and reached the same result.

"I thought, 'Man, this is easy.' Well, I shouldn't say easy. It wasn't as difficult as I thought it would be," McCormick says.

In high school, McCormick was one of California's best pitchers. His father, Kenneth, was a semipro baseball player whose dreams of a major-league career were interrupted by World War II. Having a left-handed son, McCormick's father saw how his son could achieve the dream denied to him. When McCormick was seven or eight years old, Kenneth built a mound in the family's backyard in the Mojave Desert and taught his son how to pitch.

"He relived his whole life through me," McCormick says. "He wanted to be a ballplayer. He was scouted by the St. Louis Browns. He was a right-handed pitcher, but that was World War II. So, he got married and went off to the military, and when he came back he was married now and had one or two kids and needed to make some money.

**Bonus baby Mike McCormick. Courtesy of the National Baseball Hall of Fame and Museum, Cooperstown, N.Y.**

There was too much risk in being a D ballplayer. He didn't know if he would be cut or wouldn't be cut, so along came me, and I was left-handed."

McCormick credits his father with teaching him the basics, but he denies his dad made him a major leaguer.

"Athletes are born. They're not really made. You can't just take somebody and say, 'I'm going to make them a major-league player.' He put the spit shine on me."

McCormick demonstrated this ability by always playing against older competition.

"I was playing American Legion ball when I was in eighth grade. I was playing against freshmen, seniors in high school. But, I didn't have any option—there were no other organized leagues in place yet, so I played American Legion. I played left field when I didn't pitch. I was a good hitter, hit third, fourth, or fifth, somewhere in that part of the lineup. And [when pitching], I always got a lot of strikeouts."

By the time McCormick was in high school, his family had moved from the Mojave Desert, a remote setting where McCormick could take his .22 and shoot it away from the house and risk hitting no one or nothing, to Pasadena, California. He played baseball at Mark Keppel High School in Alhambra. He played well enough for the local minor-league team, the Hollywood Stars, to take him under its wing and invite him to Gilmore Field in Los Angeles to throw batting practice and give him a jersey and a glove and other perks.

He played well, winning 34 games for his high school team and 49 for his American Legion team. Yet big-league scouts didn't notice McCormick until he was selected for the New York–California All-Star Game, the teams composed of the best amateur players from each state. He traveled to New York City and played the game at the Polo Grounds in front of 30,000 fans. He pitched three innings and struck out all nine hitters he faced.

His performance caught the attention of New York Giants owner Horace Stoneham. Watching the game in the stands, Stoneham turned to his general manager and said, "Who is this McCormick kid?"

Nobody had an answer. The Giants' primary West Coast scout was Dutch Reuther, a former big-league pitcher who was 65 years old at the time. Reuther didn't have a scouting report on McCormick. "Here I've been player of the year for two years in the state of California, my junior and senior year in what is, at the time, considered the hub of amateur baseball, the West Coast."

McCormick attributes Reuther overlooking him to Reuther's age. "He probably missed a lot of guys."

McCormick's pitching put the Giants in motion. They offered him a signing bonus of $50,000. McCormick was flattered by the money, but he wanted to sign with the Pittsburgh Pirates, the parent team of the Hollywood Stars. But at the end of the day, the Giants presented the best offer. McCormick accepted.

Because he received a bonus of $50,000, McCormick was a "bonus baby." Under Major League Baseball's rules at the time, if a team signed a player to a contract in excess of $4,000, the team was required to place the player on its big-league roster. By design, the Giants and McCormick agreed he should join the team toward the end of the season when the team expanded its roster from 25 to 40 players. That way, they avoided any hard feelings with a young kid barely out of high school taking a job from a veteran who had been scrapping to keep his roster spot. Accordingly, McCormick signed his contract on August 31, 1956, with the Giants promising to pay his bonus in thirds. In retrospect, McCormick learned this was because the club didn't have the money to pay it in one lump sum along with his salary, $6,000 annually. "That's beer money for guys who play today."

Meanwhile, Dutch Reuther began visiting McCormick on weekends. Conversations ranged from Reuther trying to teach McCormick his pickoff move, which McCormick says was so unorthodox that he would've broken his back trying to use it, to Reuther offering to sell McCormick a diamond engagement ring.

"His wife had died, and I guess he was thinking it was too good of a ring to bury it with her. So, he didn't. He offered to let me buy it, but I didn't take him up on it. It was a beautiful ring, though."

Joining the team, McCormick was out of his element. His teammates were older than he. After a game, they would return to their wives and families or go out for a few drinks. Neither option was available to him, so he found himself alone most of the time. He walked the major-league cities, finding movie theaters and passing the time by watching films.

He was also the subject of ribbing because of his bonus.

"I got a lot of cute, smart remarks around the league when they see you the first time. Called me Jingles. I remember the first day I was in uniform. I wasn't playing, but we were playing the Dodgers. I'm catching, shagging with the infielders. Gil Hodges comes walking up behind me. Big hands, grabbed my arm and said, 'Ah, so this is what they gave that big money to.' And then just kept walking."

The team attempted to place McCormick with a mentor, making his roommate for road trips Bucky Walters, his pitching coach. "He was 60 years old. He was my dad's age."

In the big leagues, McCormick was surprised at how rudimentary accommodations were for players when they traveled.

"I'm from California. I've never heard of humidity. But you get to some of these cities, and it's so hot and humid, and the hotels don't have air conditioning. I'd ask guys, 'How do you sleep like this?' They told me what you do is you take your top sheet. Run it under cool water in the bathtub and lightly wring it out. Then you lay down under it, and it cools you off, and you go to sleep. But it's so different today, how players travel with suites and everything's first class."

Pitcher Johnny Antonelli, *The Sporting News* National League Pitcher of the Year in 1954 and the Giants' best pitcher, guided McCormick. At the Giants' anniversary celebrating 50 years in San Francisco, McCormick sought out Antonelli.

"John," McCormick said. "We roomed together for three years, and I never told you this, but I'll tell you now. All of the social skills, all of the qualities I have, whether they are good or bad, I attribute to you."

Stunned, Antonelli teared up.

McCormick explained, "You taught me how to eat. You taught me how to dress. You taught me, socially, how to be a big-leaguer. Because, all I was was this 17-year-old kid. Had two shirts. Two pairs of pants. Two socks. What do you have in high school? You're lucky if you have that."

Manager Bill Rigney brought McCormick along slowly, to some extent. In 1957, McCormick primarily pitched middle relief, and he threw only 74 innings. As he acclimated to the big leagues, McCormick liked how Rigney handled him, but, as McCormick developed into one of the National League's best pitchers, he saw deficiencies in how Rigney used a pitching staff.

"He was a difficult guy to pitch for. He had a 10-man staff, and he would try to win the pennant with six pitchers. Four guys didn't get much work, and the other six guys would get worked to death, and it showed up in September."

After McCormick's three-up, three-down debut success against the Phillies, Rigney promptly advised McCormick he was starting two days later against the Phillies. This was a mistake.

"If he would've just given me the ball before the game and said, 'You're pitching. Go warm up,' I'd been fine. But instead, he told me and gave me two or three days to think about it. And then I got nervous. I always had good control, but it wasn't so good that particular day."

McCormick pitched into the second inning against the Phillies, giving up three hits and four walks before Rigney brought in a reliever. But in time, McCormick developed into one of the best left-handed pitchers in the National League. By 1958, as a 19-year-old, he threw eight complete games. In 1959, he pitched over seven innings of no-hit ball against the Phillies (May 14). In 1960 and '61, he was named to the National League All-Star teams, and, in 1960, he had the lowest earned-run average in the National League.

"I was one of the best pitchers of my time," McCormick says. "Not the best. But one of the best."

In his two All-Star Games, he threw a combined 5 1/3 innings and gave up only one earned run, a home run to Harmon Killebrew in McCormick's hometown field, Candlestick Park.

"What was interesting about it was they moved the game up an hour for East Coast TV. The wind hadn't started to blow yet. And Killebrew hit one of those towering high fly balls the way he hit them, and the left fielder went back and put his hand on the fence to try and catch it. Had the wind been normally blowing, our shortstop would've caught it."

McCormick says he was good because he had a major-league fastball and a good curveball he could throw for strikes. "I threw strikes. A good game for me was to throw 90 good pitches in nine innings. I wanted low walks. A bad game for me was throwing 125 pitches or more."

Describing his style as a young pitcher, McCormick uses the word "cute." "In high school, I was overpowering. But in the pros, I was cute. And [after I hurt my shoulder], I just learned how to be cute another way. But the thing that made me successful, other than when I was hurting, was control."

As McCormick developed into one of the National League's best pitchers in the early 1960s, baseball was different compared to today with multimillion-dollar contracts, which, managed smartly, can mean lifetime security for the player and his family and allow him to devote his offseason to training, conditioning, and preparing for the upcoming year. During his offseasons, McCormick worked at a sporting goods store. He did this to pay the bills. After work, he jogged or played basketball to stay in shape.

Just as the Giants assembled a pennant-winning team in 1962, McCormick injured his shoulder so severely he was limited to pitching only 98 innings.

"That's the frustration of my career. I was the youngest guy to 50 wins, although I think Dwight Gooden may now hold that record. I had the record for the most wins as an 18-year-old. I was going into '62 as the ace, and it was a real disappointing year not to be a bigger part of the season. I didn't get to pitch in the World Series."

Another frustration: Nobody could tell him what was wrong with his shoulder.

"Instead of being really fluid, to protect it, I became a short-armer. I couldn't warm up in an instant."

Then he received another shock: In December 1962, the Giants traded him to the Baltimore Orioles.

"I thought the world was coming to an end."

## A NEW CHAPTER, A NEW BEGINNING

Shortly after the trade, an older friend invited McCormick to lunch and asked how he was doing. McCormick admitted the trade bothered him, that the Giants no longer wanting him left him moping around.

The older friend encouraged McCormick to change his perspective. He said, "You know, you have to look at it this way: The Giants got rid of you. But, the Orioles *got* you. Somebody wanted you."

McCormick says, "At that time, they didn't know if I was done or not. But another team wanted me just as bad as another team wanted to get rid of [me]. So, look at it that way. That's a business logic. He was right."

One immediate positive from the move was improved medical care. The team sent McCormick to Johns Hopkins Hospital for a shoulder examination.

"Back then, the medical care wasn't as advanced as it is now. All they could do is X-ray, but nothing shows up on an X-ray unless you have a chip. Or a spur. But they gave me a couple of cortisone shots, and I was okay. I mean, I still had to build my arm back up."

In Baltimore, he faced heady competition in young, fresh arms like Jim Palmer and Dave McNally. As a result, he soon found himself in the minor leagues.

"They called me in to tell me they needed me in Rochester to work. And, in essence, what they were telling you is, we got to find out if you can pitch. So, I went to Rochester, and I was just a mediocre pitcher for the first half of the year. And then, in the second half, I started to pitch really well. I don't remember my record. Maybe 14–8. And everybody says, 'Gee, that's really good.' And, I always look at it like, 'Yeah, that is good, but not good compared to where I came from. I'm an ex-big-leaguer. I should have a better record.'"

With Baltimore having an abundance of young pitchers, the team traded McCormick to the Washington Senators where George Susce redirected the course of McCormick's career by showing him the screwball. And McCormick's workload increased. From 17 innings with the Orioles in 1964 to 158 with the Senators, McCormick offered jack-of-all-trades versatility for manager Gil Hodges, starting (throwing a two-hit shutout on July 18, 1965) and relieving (earning one save in 23 relief appearances) with effectiveness. His next year with the Senators, he pitched 216 innings, won 11 games, and posted a 3.46 earned-run average. Seeing a solid pitcher who could plow through innings, the Giants brought McCormick back for the 1967 season.

## WINNING

McCormick learned he won the Cy Young Award on Halloween. He received a phone call while passing out candy to neighborhood children.

In response to his award-winning season, the Giants offered him a $5,000 raise.

McCormick wanted a $25,000 raise.

He stood firm, and he received the amount he wanted.

Similarly standing up for what's right, McCormick served as a player representative in the Major League Baseball Players Association most of his career.

"A lot of guys didn't want to have to deal with and confront management, which is what my job was. I had to take the problems that the players surfaced and go speak to the owner or the general manager. A lot of guys just wanted to play, and they didn't want to be bothered by that."

Issues McCormick and the players association pushed for included free agency and an improved pension plan.

"The pension plan was kind of in its early stages, but the free agency, they [the owners] just turned their ear off. Because we asked for just anything. Give us anything. Free agency after 10 years. After five years. All kinds of suggestions. Case dismissed. Wouldn't talk about it. Now look at it. The players have total control. And we were just asking for a little leeway."

The owners were even obstinate against one of their colleagues, Charlie Finley, owner of the Kansas City then Oakland A's.

"He wanted us to play the All-Star Game at night. Play World Series games at night. Where are we now? He was an innovative guy."

McCormick remembers Finley's proposal to use orange baseballs— the increased visibility would be better for the players and the fans— they'd be able to see the ball better. But the horsehide and the dye didn't blend well, making the ball too slippery to use.

## OPENING DAY?

As Opening Day of 1968 approached, manager Herman Franks spoke with McCormick about who would be the Opening Day starter.

"You just won the Cy Young Award—you think you would be the Opening Day starter. But Herman said something to me about [Juan] Marichal getting his nose out of joint if he weren't the Opening Day starter. So, he asked me if it would be okay with Marichal getting the start. I said, 'Why are you asking me? You're the manager. Do what you want.'"

Marichal, the best pitcher McCormick ever saw with his ability to pitch from four different arm angles yet able to control the ball from any of them, pitched Opening Day. The Giants won.

McCormick pitched the next day against the Pirates, facing Bob Veale. McCormick threw *13* complete innings, gave up only run, yet ended the day with a no-decision.

"That pretty much sums up that season." McCormick was pitching well but not getting the run support or the same timely defense behind him. He still won 12 games and posted a 3.58 earned-run average, but his numbers weren't the same as his Cy Young–winning season.

Unfortunately, in 1969, McCormick suffered a back injury that led to the end of his baseball career. Teammate Willie McCovey won the Most Valuable Player Award that season, but McCormick recalls little of McCovey's performance because he was preoccupied by his injury.

"All the problems I had had and overcome, then my back starts bothering me. So, I was probably more engrossed in my own condition than what was going on."

By 1971, he had retired from playing baseball and transitioned to a career in sales, selling copiers and printers for 30 years.

McCormick remained an athlete, specializing in long-distance running. He ran in multiple half-marathons and two marathons (Sacramento and Santa Fe). He says the most difficult thing athletically he's done is run marathons.

"We had a group at the office that just decided one day: Let's try a marathon. So, we bought the *Runner's World*, which was a magazine, and it had day one, day two, 90 days, I think, to train you for what exactly you should do if you're going to run a marathon. This day you run a mile. The next day you run five miles. It kept changing. It was tough. But then, it became easy for me to go out and run 10 miles. That was my workout: run 10 or 12 miles."

McCormick continued to jog five or six miles daily into his 70s, but he has cut back jogging because he has Parkinson's disease, which affects his balance and has caused a couple of nasty falls.

McCormick also enjoys golf ("I'm not playing well, but I really enjoy it").

In 2014, McCormick moved outside of Charlotte, North Carolina, near Lake Norman. In his new house, he has a man cave where he displays treasures from his baseball career and watches Giants games.

"All my life, you could walk into my house and you wouldn't know an athlete lived there. Stuff in boxes in the garage. And I've got a lot of it. So, I took one room, and it's completely covered with baseball stuff."

He makes occasional trips to the West Coast to catch a Giants game and visit with teammates Mays and McCovey. He also enjoys movies and time with his six grandchildren.

When asked if today's game is better, McCormick says it's different.

"I don't know about the play being better, but the conditions should make the play better. The lights are better. The gloves are better. Everything that has to do with the offensive side of the game, including the stadiums, is better. I mean, I look at some of those old stadiums when I broke in. Catchers used to wrap their fingers with tape so you'd see their fingers."

Looking back, McCormick has no regrets. "I'd do it all over the same," he says. "The only difference would be my health. My fastball, my curveball, just healthy, to see what I'd done."

# 3

# A DIFFERENT APPROACH: RANDY JONES

## 1976 NATIONAL LEAGUE CY YOUNG AWARD

*Randy Jones suggested we meet at Petco Park for our interview. So, before the Padres played the Colorado Rockies in a Saturday afternoon game, I stood by the VIP gate to connect with Randy. In his blue jeans and cowboy boots, Jones strode through the gate and was pleasant and gracious to everyone he saw, saying hello and sharing a kind word to the gate attendants, the reporters in the press box, and those working in the private box where we sat for an hour before the game started and looked back 40 years prior to when Jones was named the National League's best pitcher.*

At San Diego Padres home games, you see Randy Jones. A display in the team museum memorializes his eight seasons with the Padres, his 1,766 innings pitched, the most in team history.[1] The museum also houses the 1976 National League Cy Young Award Jones earned.

Walk around Petco Park's concourse amid its white structural beams and craft beer stands, and Randy Jones's BBQ stands serve hot dogs and brisket from the grill.

Listen to Padres broadcasts, and, pregame, Jones reviews the opposing hitters and offers insights about pitching strategy.

And look at the stands; you may spot Jones wearing his camouflaged Padres cap, sipping a Cherry Coke, and munching on a slider.

"They take care of me here," Jones says as he's handed a plate.[2]

No wonder why. True, he's a Padres legend, the first Padres pitcher to pitch in an All-Star Game, the first Padre to win a Cy Young Award. But he's well liked because he treats everyone well. Stepping onto the elevator to go up to the press box, he asks the attendant, "Dave, how are you today?"

"Oh, you know. Up and down," the attendant deadpans.

Jones laughs and pats Dave on the back. He exits the elevator and passes the dining room where scouts huddle, munching on omelets and sipping coffee. "Hey, how are you?" he calls to the workers behind the counter.

"Hey, Randy!"

He steps into the glass box overlooking the field, three tiered rows of seats where reporters and broadcasters in knit shirts peck at laptops or phone screens.

"Hey, Chris!" Jones says. "Where are you going to be today?"

"On the field, Randy."

"Good. Good. That's where you belong." He pauses. "Where's Bob? Oh, hey, Bob. Let's do this."

"This" is Jones's analysis of the opposing team's hitters, their strengths and weaknesses, and approaches the Padres' pitcher should use to achieve success. Or, as Jones downplays, "some bullshit I make up" for the Padres' pregame show.

However you put it, Jones is the San Diego Padres, through and through. Even more than 40 years after being recognized as the best pitcher in the National League.

## A DIFFERENT APPROACH

Some pitchers achieve success with power, blasting the ball past hitters. Dean Chance and Dwight Gooden come to mind, firing baseballs with blazing speeds—intimidating and unhittable.

But there are other ways to skin a cat. In college, Jones lost his velocity. The fastest he could throw was 85 miles per hour, so he couldn't overpower hitters. But he could rely on his God-given ability to place the baseball where he wanted it. Mix in changing speeds, dropping the 85 down to 70, and adapting to hitters' weaknesses and avoiding their strengths, and Jones found ways to get batters out.

"I made a living out of people's weaknesses," Jones says. "I studied it from 60 feet and six inches," he says. "Let me face a guy two or three times, and I already knew. And he's not going to change that much over the course of 10 years. And he didn't. And if I made a mistake, usually, I had to pay for it. You know, a dinger or a ball off the wall."

His reduced speed sent some batters into fits. Pete Rose once described Jones's fastball as traveling 27 miles per hour. Rose even invited Jones to move down from the pitching mound and onto the grass, closer to home plate, so the ball could reach the hitter more quickly. Jones took the jabs in stride.

"As long as you were 0-for-4, I didn't give a fuck what you said," Jones says. "I didn't care. And, the more pissed they got, the harder they would swing."

His approach evolved, especially when he introduced the sinker into his repertoire. Warren Hacker, the Padres' minor-league pitching instructor, taught Jones the pitch during spring training in 1973.

"I had a good tailing fastball and great control, but I really didn't have the sinker until then," Jones says. "Being a natural left-hander and turning the ball over all the time anyway, he just kind of got me rolling over on the baseball. I started playing around with it. Say, two weeks later, I was throwing a bullpen, and, all of a sudden, that was the first time I had seen it sink."

The ball didn't just sink—the bottom fell out of it.

Jones remembers thinking, "What the hell was that?" Seeing the drop encouraged him to continue tinkering with the pitch.

"It was kind of like finding a new toy," he says. "Then I found I could change speeds with it. Then, it would sink even a little more. And that was just by the old adage of, if you want to throw a changeup, drag your back foot more. So, that's what I started doing. I started using my back foot to change speeds on the sinker. It was the same technique I had been doing in college, except I had this new weapon that had more tilt to it. It sank instead of just tailing off the plate or on the corner. Then I realized it wasn't the swings and misses I was looking for. I was looking for contact. And I bought into it real quick."

With the sinker, hitters were confounded: Should they take a pitch that looks like a ball, or should they start swinging at a pitch that they suspect may drop for a strike?

The pitch produced excellent results for Jones, and it reminds him of one of the 1970s premier power hitters, Greg Luzinski.

"Greg had an uncanny knack of coming up to the plate with a runner on and no outs," Jones says. "I never seen a guy hit a better double-play ball in my life." He laughs. "It took him 10 seconds to run to first."

Luzinski came up to the plate once after Mike Schmidt reached base on a hit. No outs, and Jones smiled at Luzinski from the mound.

"You motherfucker," Luzinski said.

"He knows that I know he's going to hit a fucking ground ball," Jones says. "And, the second sinker ball, I swear to God, he hit like a three-hopper to the shortstop. I just remember I spun around and said, 'Run, Greg, run!'"

The ribbing was good natured. After that game, Jones dropped by the Holiday Inn bar, just across the street from Veterans Stadium. He spied Luzinski and Phillies teammate Garry Maddox in a booth. He bought them a round of drinks.

"Who ordered these?" Luzinski asked.

The bartender pointed to Jones. "Randy did."

"Oh, Jesus! Get over here!"


## FIGURING THINGS OUT

Jones spent his first season in the big leagues in 1974. He led the league in losses with 22. He recognized he needed to make some changes.

"One thing about losing 22 in '74: how many games I was in until the sixth inning. I was right there. We would be tied. And then, all of a sudden, I didn't realize I was getting tired, and I was elevating the baseball. And once you elevate a sinker, it won't sink. It just tails, and I'd get beat."

After the season, Jones reflected and realized he needed more strength to have endurance to pitch late into games. So he started running more. With more endurance, his record improved in '75. He also worked with a new pitching coach, Tom Morgan, who suggested some fundamental changes to Jones's delivery: keeping his front shoulder in and following through with his pitches, his head down toward home plate.

"And I threw everything over a stiff front leg," Jones says. "It was, bend, and then I would get over my front leg, and then I would throw everything against a stiff front leg. That was my timing. I would stiffen up, and I knew right where the release points were for all the pitches. I knew what to do, and the feel was just uncanny. That was really the big thing."

With the adjustments, Jones saw successful results.

"He helped me pitch deeper into games. I was throwing a little across my body for deception, but he stopped that. He wanted a cleaner follow-through of the pitch."

Jones found he enjoyed working a quick pace. One game in 1975 lasted only 97 minutes. Jones pitched all eight innings and threw a miniscule 68 pitches.

"I worked fast and was confident and pounded the strike zone," he says. "A tempo really helped me. I liked the feel. And, also, it made a hitter uncomfortable. I have guys get in the box, and they look up, and I'd be halfway through my windup. They're going, 'Jesus, what the hell's going on?'"

And Jones posted the National League's lowest earned-run average, 2.24, won twenty games, and was named to the All-Star team. But, he finished second in Cy Young Award voting to the New York Mets' Tom Seaver.

Jones was thinking he could do better.


## CLEAR EXPECTATIONS

Coming close to winning the Cy Young Award in 1975 helped Jones focus on a goal for the upcoming season: win the Cy Young.

"In the back of my mind, coming in second to the Cy Young Award kind of left a bad taste in my mouth," Jones says. "And I knew mentally that I could win that Cy Young Award. Physically, I didn't know, but mentally, I knew I could do it."

After the 1975 season, Jones took it easy through the holidays. He traveled and appeared at banquets and speaking engagements, Southern California's and San Diego's sports hero. But on January 2 ("I had a little hangover on January 1," he says with a laugh), he started running, usually five to six miles each day. He mixed up the routine by going to a

**Intent on the Cy. Courtesy of the National Baseball Hall of Fame and Museum, Cooperstown, N.Y.**

football field and tossing a football with a friend ("We would run pass patterns and just get your cardio in"). After five days of running, he started playing catch "all of the time." A week later, he transitioned to the mound.

Before leaving for spring training, Jones met with general manager Buzzy Bavasi to discuss a contract for 1976. Negotiations were smooth. Both sides quickly agreed to a one-year deal for $65,000. And, as thanks for Jones's great work in 1975, Bavasi bought him a new Chevy Blazer.

When he reported to spring training, Jones met his new pitching coach, Roger Craig, the native North Carolinian who spent 12 years pitching in the big leagues, beginning with the Brooklyn Dodgers in 1955. Craig asked how he could best help Jones. Jones looked at him and said, "Give me the ball every fourth day. That's a good start."

Craig said, "You got it."

As the season progressed, Jones was grateful to work with Craig.

"He was really good as a mental motivator and keeping you positive."

Like on Opening Day: Craig kept Jones on an even keel. The Padres hosted the Atlanta Braves at Jack Murphy Stadium before a sold-out crowd. Jones stepped from the dugout to head to the bullpen to warm up. Craig walked beside him. Halfway to the bullpen, Jones realized the crowd was standing up and cheering for him.

"It just freaked me out," he says. "I had chills."

Then Craig nudged Jones.

"Look, Randy," Craig said. "They remember me. They still love me!"

"I started laughing," Jones says. "I started laughing my ass off. He knew what to say, and that broke the ice."

Though Jones laughed before that start, he spent most of the season focused and in the zone.

"I was really locked in. I mean, I couldn't believe how quiet it was out there on the mound," Jones says. "In my own little world. And I knew what I had to do, and more times than not, went out there and executed. If somebody made an error, I didn't get upset. I would just bear down even more to get the next out."

Although he was excited to start the season and had high expectations for himself, Jones was out of rhythm during the first part of that Opening Day game.

"I lost the feel. I walked a guy. And I was kind of scuffling with my location, and I wasn't happy about it. I couldn't quite get into a groove."

But during the first inning, Braves baserunner Jerry Royster took a lead off first. Jones glanced over, lifted his leg, then turned and fired to first and picked Royster off.

"That was a turning point right there," Jones says. "Because, when I picked that guy off, it all clicked, and I wound up going nine."

Indeed, Jones went the distance and earned the win. By the end of April, he had won four games and earned National League Pitcher of the Month honors. In May, he won six more and collected the monthly award again. At the end of June, his record was 14–3, and there was talk he would be the first pitcher since Denny McLain to win 30 games in a season. Jones did his best to keep the hype and the talk of achievements out of his mind and to focus on pitching. Like in June when he tied the record for most innings pitched (68) without issuing a walk.

"I was just in a groove and pitching and doing my thing," Jones explains. "I think I was at maybe 56 innings [without issuing a walk], and goddamn Roger Craig had to bring it up. I didn't even know it. I was just cruising along and winning ballgames. If he hadn't told me, shit, I'd've gone 100. And then it's in the back of your mind, you know what I mean? That was hilarious. I didn't want to know. I wasn't paying attention. I was just pitching."

After he walked Marc Hill and tied Christy Mathewson's record, Jones joked with Craig.

"Next year, when you look in the record book, it's going to say Christy Mathewson and Randy Jones. That's really going to make me look fucking good. That's better than being by myself," Jones said.

"Damn, you're right!"

In terms of keys to success, Jones points to a couple of factors. One was his control. If an umpire was calling pitches slightly off the plate as strikes, Jones zeroed in on this area as his target. Second, he pitched to contact. He didn't want a high pitch count and a lot of strikeouts. He was content with three pitches and three groundouts to get out of an inning. And he liked working with his catcher, Fred Kendall, who caught all but one of Jones's starts in 1976. Combining Jones's control with Kendall's positioning behind the plate, Kendall rarely had to move his glove to catch the ball. And the two were in sync in terms of pitch selection.

"I didn't like shaking him off," Jones says. "I'd be thinking of a pitch, a slider, and you know, like working backwards. I might be 2–0, say, and I feel like throwing a slider right now. And he'd put the slider down. I don't know why. I was like, 'Son of a bitch.' It's the way we worked. And

I got to the point where it was just automatic. He'd put it down, and I would pitch. It made my life easier."

With Jones preferring to work at a quick pace, he didn't like a lot of visits from his catcher. And he certainly didn't like group meetings with infielders huddled around the mound when manager John McNamara walked out there to talk with Jones.

"I'd run them all off," Jones says. "'Get the fuck out of here. He doesn't want to talk to you. If he wants to talk to you, he'll come over to your spot.' That's the way I was. I tuned everybody else out except for Freddy. I talked to Freddy, and that was it."

Jones praises Kendall for picking the right times to take a break and talk to his pitcher.

"When the adrenaline starts flying and you start competing, I always had a tendency to rush a little bit. I would get too fast. I would dig in to the hitter and start rushing, and my arm would drag a little bit. And, all Freddy had to do, he would squat down and [signal to slow down]. You could see it. Stay back. You're rushing again. And, I'd go, 'All right.'"

Sometimes, Jones would call time just to have fun with his catcher. Kendall would reach the mound and lift up his mask and ask, "What's the matter?"

"Do you see the blonde in the third row?"

As Kendall turned to look, Jones stopped him. "Don't look now, goddamnit! Look when you're walking back. Don't make it so obvious."

Meanwhile, pitching coach Craig wanted to know what the battery was discussing, so he ambled out to the mound.

"What's up?" he asked.

"I just asked Freddy if he'd seen the blonde in the third row up," Jones answered. "Behind the plate."

"Where?" Craig asked, turning to look for the third row.

"Not now!" Jones said. "Be discreet!"


## STAYING SHARP

Throughout 1976, Jones adhered to a routine. On days he pitched, he typically piddled around his house.

"I was outside working in the yard," he says. "Not killing myself, but working in the yard, keep[ing] my mind busy."

He trimmed shrubs, planted plants, pruned fruit trees. Sometimes, he would get the itch to redesign his landscape. Or install a sprinkler system.

The day after he pitched, he rested. The next, he pitched a bullpen.

"I never had a start, I don't care if it was a 10-inning one-hitter, the next time I got on the mound for my bullpen, every time there was something I needed to work on and get better at. Every single time. There was not one time that I hit that mound very composed and happy about the last time out there. There was something I didn't like. And I would go out there and work on it until I was happy with it."

Specifically, during his bullpen, he concentrated on throwing strikes to different locations in the zone. He didn't just toss a few sliders to watch them slide or curveballs to watch them drop. He focused on *where* they landed.

"There's a spot in the strike zone that, nine out of 10 times, I know I can hit it," Jones says. "And, it was down and away to a right-hander or down and in to a left-hander. And that's what I worked on."

Another constant was running. In between starts, Jones sprinted from foul line to center field, walked back, and sprinted again. And again. And again. Jones was and is a believer in repetition, something he learned from his high school baseball coach Don Terranova, who watched as Jones practiced his delivery time after time; if it was slightly off, Terranova made him do it again until it was right. For example, if Jones practiced 100 wind-ups, when he was finished, Terranova would say, "You screwed up 36 of them. You owe me 36 more."

"He taught me," Jones says. "Pay attention and don't half-ass it."

Comparing this approach that led to success in the mid-1970s with today's game, Jones says nowadays teams want pitchers with firepower. Which is fine. But he suggests that some alternatives produce success, too.

"Why not get creative where you can find that one little niche where you can sandwich him in, a guy who's got great control, good command, knows how to get people out. Pretty simple shit. That's what I would do. . . . All you got to do is get them on their front foot, and the ball's not there yet. I mean, that's really what it was all about. What are you going to do? This ball is sinking, and you're already on your front foot? You're going to hit a ground ball! You've got no choice. It's got to go to the ground. It's not rocket science."

## SETBACKS

In August 1976, Jones was involved in a serious car accident. Headed home after a road trip to Atlanta, he was driving his 240Z at 3:30 in the morning. Irritated about a close loss, he sped down the highway. Jones moved to pass a car, but his speed scared the other driver, who wound up blocking Jones. To avoid hitting the other car, Jones spun into a telephone pole. He wound up with cuts, bruises, and stitches. He didn't miss a start, though. In fact, he went on to pitch seven more complete games, including a shutout of the Expos on August 27.

During his last start of the season against Cincinnati, his 40th after already pitching 314 innings, he tore the nerve attached to his biceps tendon.

"My arm was tired," Jones says. He had thrown 25 complete games that season to lead the National League. He wasn't feeling good during warm-ups, but he didn't want to miss a start. Then, in the second inning while facing Bill Plummer, Jones threw a pitch that didn't feel right.

"It was just like a little throb pain."

Jones kept pitching. Cesar Geronimo hit a groundball to shortstop for the first out of the inning. But his arm didn't feel right. Jones stood on the mound, and John McNamara came out and asked him what was wrong.

"I've got to shut it down," Jones said. "Something's not right."

So Jones returned to the clubhouse, iced his arm, and rested. After three days, the soreness persisted. He then met with orthopedic surgeon Frank Jobe in the Padres' training room. While Jones and teammate Doug Rader talked about fishing during the offseason, Jobe asked Jones to make a muscle in his left arm.

Jones flexed and kept talking about fishing.

Jobe repeated, "Make a muscle for me."

Jones said, "I am." He looked down and saw no bicep.

At first, doctors believed Jones tore his tendon. He went in for surgery to reattach it, but Dr. Jobe recognized that the tendon was fine and saw that a nerve was snapped.

"We can't fix that," the doctor said. "It's still in the nerve canal, but it's got to grow back on its own."

Jones rested and waited, then rebuilt the muscle, using small weights. By April 1977, he was back on the mound. But he subsequently tore the nerve multiple times during his career, and, after the 1982 season, he hung up his cleats and retired from playing.

## COACHING

Jones remained in the San Diego area, and he taught pitching lessons. Joe Zito, a musician, contacted Jones and arranged for the Cy Young Award winner to work with Zito's teenage son, Barry.

"We worked on his fundamentals, on teaching him some things that should never change," Jones says.

The thing that stands out about working with the future Cy Young Award winner is teaching young Zito the importance of mental discipline. During one session, Zito told Jones that he couldn't throw a changeup.

"Bullshit," Jones said. "Throw it 600 times."

For the next hour, Zito threw one pitch—the changeup. Zito then said, "That's feeling better. Can I throw a fastball now?"

"No. Changeup."

Looking back, Jones says Zito threw close to 125 consecutive changeups, and Jones admired how Zito gritted through it.

"His desire to be the best, I hadn't seen it since my own desire. And that really inspired me. I was feeding off of what I saw in him. It reminded me of myself and how bad I wanted it. And how hard he worked. Just a good kid. Pretty quiet. Worked hard. I stayed on his ass and made him work."

After two and a half years of lessons, Jones pulled the Zitos aside.

"We're done," Jones said. "I can't teach you anything more. Now, you've just got to go do it. I'm always here for you if you have problems or something. But," Jones reminded him, "the fundamentals never change."

Zito nodded.

"Never give up on yourself," Jones said. "You've got talent. Work on it."

Now, with a smile, Jones says, "And, that's what the kid did."

## POSTPLAYING DAYS

Jones has remained busy. He's worked in catering and opened restaurants. He sells Randy Jones BBQ Sauce in Southern California grocery stores and meat markets. He organizes annual charity golf tournaments, and he's hosted a hunting show on the Outdoor Channel.

In January 2017, he announced he had throat cancer.

Six months later, he's cancer-free, but the treatments have been trying. Jones has felt locked in to beat cancer much like he felt an intensity when pitching.

"It's a focused concentration," he says. "That's what it is. Because, I might be home after radiation. And, as bad as I felt, [I'd] just get up. Instead of laying around, I'd get up and go outside. I painted the whole inside of the goddamn garage and cleaned it out. It took me two weeks. I felt awful, but goddamnit, it wasn't going to get the best of me. Fuck that shit. I'm not quitting. I wouldn't quit. . . . I would work for 20, 25 minutes. Then, I'd go sit in one of my hunting chairs, watch TV for a little bit and rest, and I'd get back up. Get back working."

Facing obstacles and overcoming them, this is familiar territory for Jones. He heard he didn't belong as a major-league pitcher, but his mastery of control led to the Cy Young Award. He tore a nerve in his pitching arm and came back to pitch another six seasons. Cancer has taken a physical toll, with Jones now weighing less than he did during his playing days, but he's pressing on . . . and prevailing.

# 4

# A SEASON FOR THE AGES: RON GUIDRY

## 1978 AMERICAN LEAGUE CY YOUNG AWARD

*It was a cool and overcast fall morning in Scott, Louisiana, when I stepped into Ron Guidry's barn. Inside, multiple hunting trophies of ducks were mounted on the walls, and Guidry knew each one of them, when he harvested them, some reaching back to his boyhood and teenage days. He mentioned that duck season had just opened and that he would be looking for a few more birds, but not just any. He would be targeting a few specific species that weren't already on his walls.*

*We sat down and began talking baseball. He brought up Ray Boudreau, who coached Guidry in high school, and Bubba Trahan, Guidry's catcher in college ("Little bitty guy," Guidry said. "About as tall as that filing cabinet."), and how they taught him some early lessons in pitching beyond throwing it faster than hitters could time and catch up with. Then he shook his head, thinking about how things have changed, how things are more accelerated today compared to when he was growing up and learning how to play.*

*"I get people, their kids are 10 years old, you know, they want me to work with them on curveballs and sliders," he says. "He's 10 years old— I don't think his arm's ready now. Give him a few more years. Wait till he gets around high school. What the hell you need a slider for? There isn't nobody can hit the ball if you throw hard. You know, things like that. When I got to American Legion, [Boudreau] was the first one that started preaching about how to use breaking balls and changeups and make the ball do something out of the ordinary. Every once in a while."*

In his fourth season in the big leagues, 27-year-old Ron Guidry won the Cy Young Award. Not only did he win, but he did so *unanimously*, earning all 28 first-place votes, the first unanimous recipient since Steve Carlton in 1972. Pitching nearly flawlessly, Guidry led the league in wins (25), shutouts (nine), earned-run average (1.74), and winning percentage (.893).[1]

The dominance didn't happen overnight. Guidry spent parts of six years in the Yankees' minor-league system, picking up tips from coaches like Jerry Walker, who counseled Guidry to vary his speeds, to mix throwing harder with slower to throw off hitters' timing. Under Walker's tutelage, Guidry began dropping his 95-mph fastball to 90, just enough of a difference to produce a groundball or a pop-up instead of a well-hit line drive. Minor-league pitching coordinator Cloyd Boyer noticed Guidry's mechanics weren't suited to throwing a curve but encouraged him to learn another pitch, the slider. Guidry added the pitch, and he developed into an effective relief pitcher, closing games for the Triple-A Syracuse Chiefs in 1975 and '76. That success resulted in a call-up to the big club. But once he made it to the majors, opportunities were few. Yankees manager Billy Martin preferred using proven veterans rather than rookies, so Guidry's appearances were generally limited to mop-up duty in blowouts. Despite the limited chances to pitch, he took advantage of being among the best and learned from the experts around him, particularly fellow bullpenners Dick Tidrow and Sparky Lyle.

"When I got to the big leagues, that first road trip that I went on, Tidrow was my roommate," Guidry says. "You're learning, and here you have an established guy that you're actually rooming with. Well, you talk baseball all the time. I learned a lot from Dick about pitching."[2]

Lyle, winner of the 1977 American League Cy Young Award, saw in Guidry a natural throwing motion well suited for the slider, a pitch Lyle perfected during a lengthy career as a closer. Guidry had been throwing the slider for a few seasons, but Lyle saw how it could be better. He pulled Guidry aside.

"You know what?" Lyle said. "Dirt [Dick Tidrow] and I have been talking, and you need another pitch. You need a good breaking ball."

"Trust me," Guidry said. "I've been trying to throw a curveball since I was 10 years old, and it still ain't working."

Lyle shook his head. "I've been watching you throw," he said. "Other than you throwing much harder than me, we throw a lot alike. Our mechanics are a lot alike."

Lyle paused.

"I think I can show you how to throw the same kind of slider I throw."

"I'm game," Guidry said.

So Lyle mentored his young teammate and helped him fine-tune the pitch. They worked during batting practice. The two threw the baseball back and forth over the center-field grass, with Lyle suggesting a tweak here or an adjustment there. Lyle's tutoring wasn't so much in terms of teaching Guidry a new grip as it was helping him refine how he rotated his wrist when he released the ball. The revised slider improved enough that Guidry tried it out in the bullpen and on the mound to see how it looked.

It looked great. The catcher misjudged the ball's drop so poorly that he didn't catch it. The ball bounced off his shin guard instead.

Lyle looked at Guidry.

"I think you've got something there," Lyle said.

While Tidrow and Lyle helped the newcomer improve on the field, they also welcomed him as a teammate. As Guidry sat in the Yankees' bullpen for the first time, Lyle asked, "You got a nickname? What'd they call you?"

"Ronald," Guidry answered.

"Ronald? No. We don't go by first names around here," Tidrow said.

"Where are you from?" Lyle asked.

"Louisiana."

"What do they have in Louisiana?" Tidrow asked.

"Well, we've got a lot of snakes," Guidry said. "Got a lot of alligators . . ."

"Gator!" Lyle said. "That's it! You're Gator."

The next inning, Lyle continued to indoctrinate Guidry, this time by lighting his shoelaces on fire. Gator, welcome to the bullpen.

Guidry is grateful for Lyle and Tidrow's help.

"I have a guy like Tidrow who was teaching me about pitching, then I got a guy like Sparky who taught me how to throw a slider. So, you put those together, I can only get better. I can't get worse."

Although Guidry improved, it didn't translate to more appearances. In fact, Guidry yo-yoed from the big leagues to Triple A and back. The lack of opportunity frustrated Guidry to the point of walking away from baseball. After one demotion, he packed his car, and, instead of heading for Syracuse, he pointed the car for Louisiana and home.

His wife Bonnie couldn't believe his decision.

"This is the first time I'll ever have known you to quit something before you figure out if you're good enough at it," she said.

Her words made him reconsider.

He turned the car around and continued the baseball journey. With his new and improved slider, he was a mismatch in Triple A, a man against boys striking out 50 in 40 innings. He gave up only three earned runs. And, by 1977, he was with the Yankees to stay.

## JOINING THE ROTATION

When the 1977 season began, Guidry was still on shaky ground with Billy Martin. Not that Martin didn't like Guidry—it was simply a matter of Martin trusting veteran pitchers, not rookies. So Guidry would pitch in relief then languish in the bullpen for a couple of weeks before being called to the mound again.

Then the Yankees visited Seattle in late April. That's when they traded for pitcher Mike Torrez from Oakland. Torrez couldn't make it to the Kingdome for a start, and Martin needed a starting pitcher. He looked to Guidry.

"Just give me four or five good innings. That's all I need," Martin said.

"Okay," Guidry said. He headed out to the bullpen to warm up. Lyle joked with him.

"Well, you ain't pitched in two weeks," Lyle said. "So, at least you're going to be strong."

Guidry laughed. He liked how he was feeling. And the good feeling continued as he began the game. He struck out the first hitter. From the first through the fourth innings, he retired 10 consecutive hitters. By the ninth inning, he was still pitching—a shutout, in fact. But after Guidry gave up two hits, Martin walked to the mound and signaled for a relief pitcher.

**Settling in with the Yankees. Courtesy of the National Baseball Hall of Fame and Museum, Cooperstown, N.Y.**

Not bad for an emergency fill-in.

Time passed. Jim "Catfish" Hunter was scheduled to start, but his shoulder was hurting. Again, Martin looked to Guidry at the last minute. Again, Guidry pitched into the ninth inning before Martin removed him.

Next up: Don Gullett missed a start. Guidry stepped in and delivered, pitching 8 1/3 innings. The results left Martin with a new starting pitcher to add to the rotation. Pitching coach Art Fowler shared the news with Guidry. Fowler asked, "Do you think you can handle starting?"

"I've done it three times now," Guidry said. "I just want to pitch, dude."

"Well, we're going to move you to the rotation," Fowler said.

Still, Martin had doubts about Guidry's ability to finish a game. Guidry pitched three more games into the ninth, but, at the first sign of a walk or a hit, Martin called the bullpen. Until June 16 when Guidry was pitching a shutout against Kansas City. After a leadoff walk to George Brett started the ninth, Martin stepped from the dugout to remove Guidry. This time, though, catcher Thurman Munson hustled and beat Martin to the mound. Munson counseled his batterymate.

"You've got to tell him something," Munson said. "If you don't tell him something, he's gonna keep taking you out. Tell him anything you want, but just tell him something so you can finish."

Martin reached the mound.

"How you feeling?" Martin asked.

"You really want to know how I feel?" Guidry responded.

"Yeah. How're you feeling?" Martin repeated.

"I think you ought to get your ass off my mound so I can finish my game," Guidry said.

"You got it," Martin said. No signal to the bullpen. He turned around and walked back to the dugout.

Guidry then retired the next three Royals to earn the win and his first shutout in the big leagues.

Guidry finished 1977 as a starter, winning 16 games and losing seven. As he adjusted to starting, he found new routines. Pitching coach Art Fowler helped with the transition.

"He just told me if you can't throw the ball over the plate, you can't pitch in the big leagues," Guidry says. "It's as simple as that. Whatever you have, if you throw 95, I can't teach you to throw 96. If you got a nasty curveball, I can't teach you how to make it better. All I need for you to do is to take those pitches and throw the ball. Learn how to throw it over the plate. Where guys can swing at it. Or, try to get guys to swing at it. You know, I guess less is more. What I'm saying is, Art gave me the least amount of help, but he gave me more help than you realize in just by what he said. To me, that was the best advice I ever got."

Thurman Munson also helped with Guidry's settling into the rotation.

"He's one of the rare guys. He's truly one of the great catchers," Guidry says. "Getting to pitch to him, I didn't have to think about very many things other than throwing the pitch that he was gonna call, the location. You learn how to trust somebody so much that you know well."

With Munson making pitch selection easy, Guidry could go on autopilot and concentrate on executing his pitches. By him doing so, games moved briskly.

"In [1977], he found out more about me that he needed to know," Guidry says. "And, I found out about him. What we can do, what we can't do. What we want to do, what we don't want to do. See, that all fell in that time period. So, the prelude to that is what goes on in the '78 season. All of that goes to the next year."

The year 1977 ended well with the Yankees winning the World Series in six games.

And, as Guidry says, 1978 had a great outlook.

## A CHAMPIONSHIP SEASON FOR THE AGES

Guidry began the season pitching brilliantly, winning 13 consecutive games.

"I could have been better, though," Guidry says. "I shouldn't have walked so many guys. But there wasn't much more that I could do to make it any better."

While Guidry started hot, the same cannot be said for new closer Goose Gossage, who signed with the Yankees as a free agent, a six-year deal for $3.6 million. Initially, he struggled. In April, he had no saves, and he lost three games. Gossage's struggles were so severe that, one game, when Billy Martin visited Guidry on the mound to bring in Gossage, Guidry balked at passing the baton.

"Hey," Guidry said to Martin. "Before you say anything more, if you plan on bringing that son of a bitch into this game here? The next time

Guidry taking advantage of the opportunity. Courtesy of the National Baseball Hall of Fame and Museum, Cooperstown, N.Y.

I'm scheduled to pitch, I'm gonna throw one pitch, and I'm gonna fake an injury, and I'm gonna walk off. Until that fuckin' guy starts getting guys out, don't plan on bringing him in anymore. I'll do my own shit."

"Okay," Martin agreed. He let Guidry finish.

Gossage, warmed up in the bullpen and ready to go, knew something was up. He called the dugout to find out what was going on. Martin said, "After the game's over, go talk to 49," referring to Guidry's jersey number.

Guidry retired the next two batters to end the game. He went to his locker, sat down, and waited for Gossage. Red faced, Gossage entered the clubhouse and stormed toward Guidry's locker.

Before Gossage reached Guidry, Guidry said, "That'll be far enough."

Gossage stopped.

"Until you start getting guys out, don't plan on coming into any more of my games. I'll take care of my own shit."

Gossage listened.

"You're right," he said. "The way I've been pitching, I wouldn't want me in those games, either."

And Gossage turned away, grabbed a beer, and went to his locker.

"That's all that happened," Guidry says. "But the message was there."

Gossage's struggles didn't last long. He went on to lead the American League in saves (27) that season. And soon, Guidry trusted the closer to end the game with a Yankees win.

"You know, you're pitching, and Martin comes out again, and I said, 'You better bring Goose in because I ain't got this guy out all day. Maybe he'll have better luck.'"

Although Guidry was getting great results, the team stalled. One factor was injuries. Chris Chambliss and Graig Nettles spent time on the disabled list. So did Catfish Hunter. The result: key players weren't on the field and making their usual exceptional contributions. Meanwhile, Boston hummed on all cylinders. By July 17, New York found itself 14 games behind the Red Sox in the American League East.

Compounding the problems, the atmosphere around the team was like a soap opera. Billy Martin, Reggie Jackson, and George Steinbrenner feuded constantly.

"All this animosity," Guidry says. "It just disrupts everybody."

Tensions burst in late July when Steinbrenner forced Martin to re-sign and replaced him with Bob Lemon. Lemon, Guidry says, was a breath of fresh air. When Lemon took over the team, he called a meeting and told the players, "Go play."

"For us who had been in turmoil for the month before that, having a guy come in there and cut it—it was short, and it was sweet," Guidry says. "It was a calming effect, and it was the best medicine for what was ailing us at the time. A manager that was just going to come in and let us play."

The Yankees responded. Injuries healed. Catfish Hunter caught fire, winning all six of his starts in August. With Lemon as manager, the Yankees won 48 games and lost only 20. And gradually, the Yankees chipped away at Boston's double-digit lead while the injury bug bit the Red Sox. Meanwhile, Guidry continued to dominate. He attributes part of his success to pitching to contact, knowing an excellent defense behind him would make plays. After all, first baseman Chris Chambliss and third baseman Graig Nettles won Gold Glove Awards in 1978.

"There were the games where you overpowered teams, so you didn't need much other stuff," Guidry says. "Well, what about the games where, you didn't overpower teams? With Graig, you weren't hesitant to throw a slider in to a right-handed batter. They hit it down the line, he's gonna catch it. If I throw a fastball away, they hit the ball right down the right-field line, Chris'll catch it. If I throw a ball right over the plate and they hit it up the middle, Bucky [Dent] or Willie [Randolph] would shag it. If I gave up a ball in the left-field, center-field gap, Mickey [Rivers would] go get it. When you know you have that behind you, you're not afraid to do anything. And, when you're talking specifically about Yankee Stadium, when I was playing there, center field was 430 [feet], okay? Hey, fastball, middle, away—you can hit it as far as you want. If you don't hit it 435, Mickey's gonna catch it. That's why you can throw more fastballs than have to worry about throwing other stuff. You can let 'em hit it! You could go out to pitch an inning and throw three pitches and get out. You throw three fly balls, 420, 419, 418—oh, they hit the dog shit out of it. Yeah, but they didn't get a base hit. You pitch to your stadium. I wasn't afraid to let 'em hit the ball."

This approach, although effective for Guidry, isn't prevalent in today's game.

"Guys are more afraid of contact today," he says. "They're trying to fool more guys, and they get more and more in trouble. Whereas look, I got a fastball. I got a great slider. But I'm gonna throw you fastballs. This is how I'm pitching. I'm gonna start you off, do what you got to do. If you ain't nothing, I ain't changing. Throw the ball over the plate. You let 'em whale on it."

That said, Guidry was so sharp in 1978 that, during some games, teams *couldn't* make contact and whale on it. They were swinging and missing. Like the game against the California Angels on June 17 when Guidry struck out 18, one shy of the major-league record at the time.

Interestingly, when he was warming up before the game, Guidry didn't feel sharp. He anticipated a short outing. He looked at Sparky Lyle and asked, "When's the earliest you've been in a game? Because man, I got nothing."

"Just go out there," Lyle assured him. "You'll be good."

Guidry started the game and immediately saw his life flash before him when Bobby Grich ripped a line drive back to the pitcher. But Guidry pressed on. He tried to pitch with what he thought was subpar stuff. He just wanted the win, but during the fourth inning, he struck out three hitters to end the inning. In the sixth inning, he struck out Dave Chalk, Joe Rudi, and Don Baylor. But he wasn't counting strike-outs—until after the seventh inning, when the scoreboard posted that Guidry had struck out 15, tying Whitey Ford's team record for the most strikeouts in a game.

That's when Guidry looked at Thurman Munson. "I got 15?"

"You have 15!" Munson said. "The major-league record is 19. We're gonna go for it."

"Whoa, whoa, whoa," Guidry said, putting on the brakes. "We need to concentrate on winning this game. We ain't worrying about no strike-outs. Call pitches to get guys out with."

"Okay," Munson agreed. "I'll give you the next inning. But if you're close in the ninth, we're gonna go for the record, or else I'm gonna break your left shoulder."

"Fine," Guidry said.

Guidry pitched the eighth inning like he had the others. He struck out Ike Hampton to bring the game's total to 16. Then he went out in the ninth inning, gunning for strikeouts. He rung up two more to end the game with 18.

Later, Guidry learned different dimensions to the story. Diane Munson, Thurman's widow, visited Yankee Stadium in 1980 on Old-Timers Day. She shared a story with Guidry about her husband after the Angels game. He came home, played with the kids and tucked them into bed, and tried to wind down. Diane fell asleep. But she woke up during the night and saw Thurman wasn't in bed. She saw him sitting down outside. She joined him.

"Is anything wrong?" she asked.

"Yeah," he said. "I can't sleep. I've been thinking about the damn game."

"What are you thinking?"

"If I had been paying attention, the kid could've had 20 strikeouts. He might've had more. There were guys we could have struck out that I called pitches to get a guy out with. If I had known what he had, I could've gave him a record."

Looking back, Guidry gets somber. "That's what he was thinking about. He was thinking about the damn record. Shit, I was happy with 15!"

Years later, Don Baylor, a California Angel during that game, joined the Yankees as a free agent. He told Guidry that the Angels, toward the end of the game, just didn't want to strike out.

"I've never been in a game like that," Baylor said. "We knew we didn't have a chance after the fourth inning. When you got into the sixth inning, everybody on the team tried *not* to strike out."

After all, their teammate was Nolan Ryan, the record-holder for most strikeouts in a game.

Baylor told Guidry, "We weren't worried about trying to win the game. We were trying not to strike out so Nolan could keep the record."

Guidry laughed.

"The most amazing thing," Baylor said, "as much as we were trying not to strike out? You were still striking us out. That was what was amazing about your game. Nobody realizes things like that."

## KEYS TO SUCCESS

Throughout the season, Guidry maintained a routine. He ran—a lot. He had a history of this. In high school, he ran distance events in track.

Then in his senior year, he switched to sprints. He credits this training for his durability. To illustrate, Guidry compares himself to Goose Gossage.

"If you ran both of us out there, sure, Goose is going to throw harder. But he's going to throw harder for three or four innings. You get him into the fifth or sixth inning, I'm gonna pass him up. Because he's gonna be tiring out. It wasn't true about me. A lot of guys said I actually threw harder in the ninth than I did in the first. Yeah. I got stronger."

For his running regimen, Guidry shagged flies during batting practice. He ran foul pole to foul pole, trying to catch everything he could for an hour.

"I just ran all the time," he says. "So, of course your cardiovascular's going to be good. Your legs are going to be strong. All I got to do is stand on the mound and throw a little ole white ball. I can do that all day."

He also took groundballs every day, usually around 50. At the beginning of his career, Guidry was motivated by self-defense.

"You can't imagine how hard that ball comes up the middle," he says. "You can get killed. There's been some serious injuries. Well, I didn't want that happening to me."

The practice paid off as Guidry won five Gold Gloves in his career.

Guidry arrived at the ballpark early, about four or five hours before the game. He would make a pot of chicory coffee, a favorite among teammates and clubhouse staff; check in with the trainers; read the papers and a chapter or two from a best-selling novel or a history book about the Civil War; and work a crossword puzzle. He relaxed, sometimes catching a nap. Sometimes, he sat behind a drum kit he kept in a spare room at Yankee Stadium and banged on the skins. ("I had been playing the drums since I was young. It kept my wrists very strong.") He would check in with the groundskeepers and share preferences on how he liked the mound, a longer or a shorter slope, depending on the time of the season and his energy level. When he was fresh, he liked a long slope. ("When you're fresh, you feel like you can go all the way to the plate. When you're tired, you can't reach far enough.")

He might eat a hot dog from the canteen, or maybe he would pass. He wasn't a fan of a big meal before games ("I didn't want to puke on national television."). And by the first pitch, he was ready to go.

Another routine he established was how he dealt with the press. While the Bronx Zoo soap opera swirled with tensions among Martin, Jackson, and Steinbrenner, three strong personalities, Guidry stayed under the radar.

"You play a game, you got the press," Guidry says. "If I talk to 'em I don't have to say a whole hell of a lot. If they ask me what I felt, it felt good. If they ask me what I thought about this, I tell 'em. Yes, no, maybe. I'll tell you what. If you got a yes, no, maybe attitude, they ain't gonna be able to write too many stories. So I learned early how to handle the press. Unless somebody hollered out my name in the locker room, why in the hell do I gotta poke my nose into somebody else's business?"

And just as he hung around with veterans like Dick Tidrow and Sparky Lyle as a newcomer, eager to absorb a lesson or two to help him improve, Guidry also looked forward to learning from Yankees coaches Yogi Berra and Elston Howard. He liked stopping by their lockers and asking questions. Until the day after he struck out 18 California Angels. That's when Guidry sat down at Berra's locker and started to ask a question and Berra stopped him.

"Jesus Christ! What more can we do?" Berra said, laughing. "How do you think you struck out 18 guys last night? You're 12–0! We can't help you anymore! Leave us the fuck alone!"

Guidry turned to Howard, who was shaking his head.

"We can't do nothing no more," Howard said, chuckling.

Looking back, Guidry smiles. "You're putting it all together. That's a lot to do with the successes or the failures that you have. The successes are because you're listening, you're paying attention. The failures are probably because you're not asking enough questions, you don't have enough answers; consequently, you're not doing the right job."

Though Berra may have kidded about no more tutoring, Guidry continued to learn about pitching from teammate Catfish Hunter. Hunter taught the importance of variety, of adapting when things aren't working at 100 percent. He counseled Guidry to think about those games when, ordinarily, he would throw 95 miles per hour but he could only get up to 92. What to do then?

Guidry waited for the advice.

"Throw a dead-fish fastball," Hunter said. "If you throw one at 85, and then throw one at 92, they won't know where to go."

Guidry agrees. "It's like throwing a great changeup when you don't have a changeup." Or, hearkening back to lessons from Jerry Walker in the minor leagues—throwing a hard slider and a softer one, a hard fastball and a slower one.

Teaching this lesson, Hunter invited Guidry to join him in the dugout and watch batting practice. Guidry obliged, and he watched the pitcher throw straight fastball after straight fastball to hitters.

"What am I looking for?" Guidry asked.

"Just watch batting practice," Hunter said.

Guidry saw the consecutive fastballs over the plate. Hitters hit some balls into the stands. Others were sharp line drives that, during a game, would be hits. But others were weak flares. Some were hit directly to where the defense would be positioned to catch them. But no hitter, even though he knew exactly what the pitcher was doing, had yet to hit 10 balls over the fence.

"Watch this next group hit," Hunter said. "Watch how many balls they actually hit that would be a hit in a game."

The lesson: You don't have to throw 95 miles per hour to get guys out. Even when hitters know what pitch is coming, you can get them out. Factor in an element of doubt, of questioning whether the pitcher will actually throw the dead-fish BP fastball or something else in his repertoire or at a different speed or in a different location, and the guesswork swings the advantage to the pitcher.

## STANDOUT MOMENTS

Guidry threw *nine* shutouts in 1978. Two were in September against the first-place Red Sox. Both were two-hitters.

The first was in Boston, a place where he enjoyed pitching but against the toughest lineup Guidry ever faced: Dwight Evans, Fred Lynn, Jim Rice, Butch Hobson, Rick Burleson, Jerry Remy, George Scott, and Carlton Fisk. With the Yankees four games behind Boston, the teams began the Fenway series with New York delivering what Guidry calls "a good ole country ass-kicking," beating Boston 15–3.

The ass-kicking trend carried over to the next game with another Yankees win, 13–2.

Now two games behind Boston, it was Guidry's turn to pitch. Starting for Boston: Dennis Eckersley.

"You got your two best pitchers going," Guidry says. "I had already won 20 games, and Eck is trying."

The two traded scoreless innings until the fourth.

"We ain't giving up," Guidry says. "We had a hero every day. It wasn't the same guy all the time. That's how our team was. If the game's close, somebody's going to step up."

After Munson led off the fourth with a single, it looked like Reggie Jackson would be the hero. He drilled a pitch down the left-field line to the warning track. Guidry figured Jackson had a cinch double and that, at a minimum, Munson would be at third base if not scoring. But Carl Yastrzemski made a backhanded catch and fired the ball to Rick Burleson, who doubled up Munson at first base. So instead of one run or two runners in scoring position, the Yankees had two outs.

But the inning wasn't over. Chris Chambliss knocked a double. Eckersley intentionally walked Nettles. Then Lou Piniella lofted a fly ball to right field that fell in between two outfielders and two infielders. Chambliss scored, opening the floodgates for the Yankees to score seven runs. With two outs.

The Sox were deflated. And Guidry nailed down the shutout. He struck out the side in the fifth and gave up no hits after the first inning.

The Yankees stayed hot and caught the Red Sox to force a one-game playoff to determine the winner of the American League East. Guidry pitched with one day less rest than usual. In the second inning, he gave up a home run to Carl Yastrzemski.

"It was just a bad pitch that got away," Guidry says. "It was one of those things."

In the bottom of the sixth, Rick Burleson led off with a double off Guidry. Jerry Remy laid down a sacrifice bunt to advance Burleson. Then Jim Rice laced a single to center, scoring Burleson and making the score Boston 2, New York 0.

"Well, it's not insurmountable," Guidry says. "We're sitting down in the dugout. We're doing what we've been doing. We just need somebody to step up. That's it. Just be patient."

Cue Bucky Dent in the seventh inning. With two men on base, he swung at a Mike Torrez pitch. Foul ball. From the on-deck circle, Mickey Rivers told Dent, "I think you might have cracked your bat." So

Rivers handed Dent his bat to use. The next pitch, Dent hit a dinger, and the Yankees went up 3–2. And the Yankees were on their way to the American League Championship Series to face the Kansas City Royals.

Looking back on the Championship Series, Guidry remembers Munson. In Game Three with the Yankees trailing 4–5 in the bottom of the eighth, Munson crushed a Doug Bird pitch for a home run to push the Yankees ahead.

"There's a couple of guys on base, guy steps up, he hasn't hit a home run in three months," Guidry says. "He hits one of the most mammoth home runs in the stadium! In the frickin' monuments! Munson. He turns it around, and you win the game."

Not only the game, but the pennant. But soon the Yankees found themselves in a familiar place where they spent most of the season: in a deficit as the Dodgers led two games to none. Before Guidry started Game Three, Munson called a team meeting, one of the few meetings the team captain called all season. He said, "This is gonna sound strange, what I'm going to say, but I'm going to say this. The Dodgers are a fairly good team, okay? And I wouldn't mind losing to them. But they're not better than us!"

The team listened.

"If Ron can win this game tonight," Munson continued, "we can win four games in a row, and this thing is over with. I'm telling you: We are so much better than them."

The Yankees responded. Guidry pitched a complete game and gave up only one run. The Yankees scored five and won. And, like Munson suggested, they went on to win the next three and claim the World Series.

Although their comeback in the American League East and beating the Dodgers in the World Series happened more than 40 years ago, deep bonds were forged. The team remains . . . a team.

"When you see 'em, you pick up where you left off," Guidry says.

## THE BOSS

Guidry played for one of the most iconic owners in sports history, George Steinbrenner.

"He was very good inside," Guidry says. "He didn't want it to be known that he was a good guy. He was hard to work for. He demanded a lot. But at the same time, he'd do anything for anybody. Especially for the team. There was nothing he didn't do for the team to make it better."

In terms of being difficult, Guidry points to Steinbrenner using the newspapers to criticize his players. Nobody wants to be criticized, and, if it needs to happen, it's usually most productive if it's a private, one-on-one conversation. But Guidry recognizes that Steinbrenner used the public barbs as a way to motivate his players.

"He would say a lot of things in the paper because he knows if you read the paper, he's going to get you to work. Because there's nothing like making him come out to be wrong."

Looking back on 19 years as a player in the Yankees organization, Guidry says Steinbrenner treated him fairly. Guidry never wanted to leave the team for a better offer elsewhere. Rumors surfaced in 1981 that the Toronto Blue Jays wanted to sign Guidry as a free agent. Guidry dismisses the rumors as a ruse to bring the Yankees to the table to work out a mutually agreeable deal before Christmas so contract negotiations wouldn't be a distraction over the holidays.

Steinbrenner was kind to Guidry's family. Before an exhibition game against Grambling University in Louisiana, only two and a half hours away from Guidry's hometown in Lafayette, Guidry's father Brolin brought his burner, pots, and some rabbits he had in the freezer. He set up a portable kitchen on the sidelines and began preparing rabbit stew before the game as a treat for Ron. Once the team showed up at the ballpark, Guidry joined his parents as Brolin cooked.

Steinbrenner pulled up in his limousine during the third inning. He mingled with the crowd and said hello to his friend, Grambling University head football coach Eddie Robinson. Guidry noticed the Boss's arrival, and he nudged his parents.

"That's Mr. Steinbrenner," Guidry said.

Steinbrenner eventually made his way to the Guidrys. Ron introduced him to his parents. They exchanged pleasantries, and Steinbrenner asked, "What smells so good?"

"Well, that's rabbit stew," Guidry said.

"That smells great," Steinbrenner said.

"It's ready if you want to try some," Brolin offered.

"Don't mind if I do."

Brolin served him a bowl. Steinbrenner took a bite, and he was hooked.

Guidry smiles. "That son of a bitch ate almost all the goddamn stew! I'm sitting down, and I'm going, 'I sure hope you're planning on sharing my dinner. 'Cause that's what they're cooking for me.'"

Steinbrenner kept eating. When he finished, he said, "Mr. Guidry, that was so good." Then he looked at Ron. "By the way. Next spring training. If you don't bring that rabbit stew, don't come."

"Okay," Guidry said.

From then on, Guidry brought a few servings of rabbit stew to Steinbrenner to begin each season. After Steinbrenner passed away in 2010, Guidry continued the tradition, sharing stew with Steinbrenner's daughter Jennifer.

## SHARING LESSONS

When Guidry was a young pitcher, he learned from Howard and Berra, Tidrow and Lyle, Walker and Boyer. A believer in paying it forward, Guidry passed on lessons learned to the next generation of pitchers, primarily during spring training but also as the Yankees' pitching coach in 2006 and '07.

"When I retired in 1989, I went in to see George," Guidry says. "He asked me to please come to spring training the next season. I said sure."

Guidry showed up to spring training for 25 seasons, happy to help wherever help was needed. If that meant working the back field with the pitchers, he was glad to do it.

One spring training, pitching coach Mark Connor asked Guidry to watch a young, slight pitcher.

"I want you to talk to him," Connor said. "He's coming back from elbow surgery, but he reminds me a lot of somebody," Connor said.

"Okay," Guidry said. And, after watching Mariano Rivera pitch, Guidry turned to Connor and said, "If he'd be left-handed, he'd be me."

"Yeah," Connor said. "That's exactly what I thought."

Guidry introduced himself to Rivera, and the two of them sat in a dugout for two hours, talking pitching. From that, the two developed a friendship so that, during spring training when pitchers needed partners to throw together, Rivera sought out Gator.

In terms of coaching, Guidry sensed a change in the game from when he played.

"The guys come along now, I actually think they think they know it all," he says. "It's harder to get them to try to do something because they're not, they might not take that advice. They want to do things their way."

As a player, though, Guidry wanted information and advice from those who came before him. It made him better. And Guidry has that extra information. He's grateful to his predecessors who shared it. After all, it helped shape him to have one of the best seasons by a pitcher and a career that made him a Yankee legend.

# 5

# THE STUDENT OF PITCHING: LAMARR HOYT

## 1983 AMERICAN LEAGUE CY YOUNG AWARD

*LaMarr Hoyt and I sat by an apartment complex's swimming pool in Columbia, South Carolina, one summer afternoon that turned to evening and talked about pitching and how he discovered what worked well from the mound and what didn't. He shared details I never thought of or appreciated before, how his pointer finger being damp could make the ball move differently compared to when his middle finger was slightly moist from sweat but the pointer was dry. In his white Chicago White Sox knit shirt, Hoyt sat in the pool chair, the water gently gurgling in the background, and he shared insight after insight. I could have listened to him for hours.*

*At one point, he nodded toward the pool. Recently, he had been in the water when some folks started tossing a football around. They threw the ball to him. He caught it and handed it to the person next to him.*

*"What are you doing?" they asked the former Cy Young Award winner who once made his living by throwing baseballs.*

*"I can't throw the ball," he said. "I wish I could."*

*Which reminded him of being invited back to Comiskey Park to throw out a ceremonial first pitch. Hoyt agreed, and his son Michael joined him. Hoyt gave the ball to his son to toss. Because the year prior, Hoyt tried to throw the ceremonial pitch. And he couldn't. The ball went five feet. Puzzled, Harold Baines, the ceremonial catcher, handed the ball back to Hoyt and asked, "What happened to your arm?"*

*Hoyt said, "When you tear three of the tendons that tie your rotator cuff together, and you've only got four of them, [and you] never had the operation, that's kind of what happens over the years."*

The first time LaMarr Hoyt faced George Brett, Brett laced a double.[1] A couple of seasons later, in 1982, Brett went 3-for-7 off Hoyt, including a home run. Frustrated, Hoyt sought advice from White Sox batting coach Charlie Lau. Lau had mentored Brett while Lau previously served as the Royals' hitting coach from 1971 through '78.

"I threw my glove in the break room, and that's where Charlie usually sat. I said, 'Okay, Charlie. You taught the son of a bitch how to hit. How do you get him out?'"[2]

"Simple," Lau explained. "He's trying to time you. The next time he comes up to bat, throw him a fastball at his eyes. Throw him a changeup in the dirt. Fastball up in his eyes and a changeup in the dirt and walk him."

Hoyt hesitated. He said, "I don't walk people." Indeed. During his Cy Young season of 1983, Hoyt's control was so precise he issued only 31 walks while pitching 260 2/3 innings.

"Walk him. Just this once. Walk him."

Hoyt followed Lau's advice. He walked Brett in four pitches.

Before Brett's next at-bat, Hoyt approached Lau. "Okay, Charlie. What do I do now?"

"Do it again."

"Do what again? Walk him? You've got to be kidding me! I don't want to walk him again!"

"Yeah," Lau said. "He's just trying to time you. You just need to throw it off a touch."

Again, Hoyt did as the coach instructed, throwing a high fastball followed by a changeup in the dirt, repeating, and walking Brett in four pitches. When Brett began grinding his bat handle, Hoyt sensed Brett was becoming frustrated.

Curious what his next step should be, Hoyt asked Lau how he should pitch to Brett for the upcoming at-bat.

"Throw him anything you want. You've got him so frustrated and so aggravated. I can see him grinding that bat. He's so pissed off, he don't know what to do."

Three pitches later, Hoyt retired Brett. "I threw him a slider, a fastball, another slider on the outside corner," Hoyt says.

The lessons learned worked perfectly in 1983 with Hoyt limiting Brett to one hit in 12 at-bats.

Throwing off hitters' timing is just one aspect of pitching Hoyt studied. Since he was a child playing Little League and his father Dewey, a former minor-league pitcher, showed him a backdoor slider, Hoyt has been intrigued with control and movement and making the ball do different things depending on the hitter and the situation. "I could talk for hours about the different philosophies of throwing balls, the different aerodynamics you can put on the ball," Hoyt says.

As a minor leaguer, Hoyt listened to fellow pitcher Michael Rusk in the Yankees' farm system. Rusk's father was a physicist, and Rusk saw pitching in aerodynamic terms.

"Rusk showed me how to manipulate the spin of the ball. If I went to my tongue with two fingers, which is legal, what I would do is wipe one finger off or wipe the other finger off. So, it depends which finger I wiped off, the ball was going which direction. If I wipe this [pointer] finger, it's a natural slider. But it's a hard natural slider. Like 95 miles per hour. And, if I wiped off this [middle] finger and this [pointer] finger was wet, the ball's going to sink, and it's going to be a very hard sinker. And that's what I used to throw Mickey Rivers all the time."

Toying with grips one day, he discovered that by adjusting his fingers and releasing the ball with a flinging motion, he could increase velocity by three or four miles per hour.

Hoyt relied on the ball's movement to keep hitters guessing. "My whole point was that, if you threw the ball, an average major-league fastball is 85, 86 miles an hour, and they only have like seven-eighths of a second to react," he says. "So, if you can cut that reaction time to say, like, two-thirds of a second or three-tenths of a second, they got no chance. And basically, that's what I worked on. Then I got it down to a fine art to where, most of the time, I would throw a fastball, but it would be moving in some direction that they didn't know where it was going. The catcher knew where it was going, but [the hitter] didn't know. But they had to commit, and it might be something that they didn't particularly want to hit."

Hoyt also looked for where he could gain an advantage. He stood on a mound with a rubber. He figured out that he needed to use the rubber as a projectile.

"The first thing I tell kids when I teach them is they put the mound up there for a reason. It's not just to let you know how far you are from the plate. It's supposed to be used as a projectile to maximize the velocity you throw to the plate. Don't pitch out of the hole in front. It puts too much pressure on your shoulder and things like that. Fundamentally, it's not the right thing to do. What you need to figure out is how to *push* off the rubber."

Through years of throwing baseballs, Hoyt found that by positioning himself in the middle of the rubber, he threw strikes consistently. "If you're on the middle of the rubber, you're directly aligned with home plate, with its center point. So, if you pitch from the middle of the rubber and you throw overhand, it's going to go right down the middle. I mean, if you don't make it move." Hoyt notes that some pitch from different sides of the rubber, but he planted in the middle because of the consistency it offered. He showcased this consistency when he pitched in front of Tony LaRussa for the first time in order to secure a roster spot on LaRussa's winter ball team in the Dominican Republic in the late 1970s.

"I told Tony to go in and get me a sanitary hose. He did, and I wrapped it around my eyes like a mask. I said, 'How many strikes do you want to see?'"

LaRussa said, "What are you talking about?"

Hoyt explained that his ability to throw strikes was based on his footwork: If he stood in the middle of the rubber, he would throw the ball right down the middle.

"So," Hoyt said, "how many strikes do you want to see right down the middle?"

"Go ahead and start."

Hoyt reeled off 10 consecutive strikes.

The next day, LaRussa called him and told him to pack his bags. Hoyt was headed to the DR for winter ball.

His love of pitching led to hours of shop talk with teammates, especially Richard Dotson, swapping tricks about throwing baseballs.

"On the nights we were off, Richard Dotson and I, we would talk about the hitters. What they liked and didn't like. What worked well for him and what worked well for me. From all that, I knew 125 hitters out of 400 in the league."

These talks were often in a hotel suite LaRussa rented for his players.

"It was frowned on for us to hang around the hotel bar," Hoyt says. "So, Tony would rent a room for us to hang out after the games. Richard and I always talked pitching. He threw one of the best changeups in the league. We're both righties, and I usually pitched first, so I could tell him throw your changeups here and here."

Though Dotson and Hoyt collaborated, they also kept some of their pitching secrets . . . well, secret. Only after both retired did Hoyt learn how Dotson threw his changeup without tipping the pitch to hitters— he held the ball with his middle, ring, and pinkie fingers and shaved eight or 10 miles per hour off its velocity while his pitching delivery continued to indicate fastball.

Hoyt said, "Damn. How come you didn't tell me that back in the day?"

Dotson responded, "Well, why didn't you tell me about your thumb on your fastball?" referring to Hoyt's method of cupping his thumb under the ball to manipulate its movement.

Just as Hoyt enjoyed analyzing how he could manipulate the ball's movement by flinging his wrist or keeping one finger damp and another dry, he liked dissecting the hitter's stance in the batter's box. In fact, sometimes he preferred not knowing anything about a hitter's tendencies (Hoyt refers to this as "going naked") and relying instead on the hitter's position in the box and knowing what Hoyt was throwing well.

"You look at the hitter. Is he looking for an inside pitch? You can tell by how he's standing in the box. So, you look at what part of the plate is available, and you give him what he doesn't want. Feed him what he doesn't want to see."

As an example, Hoyt points to the 1983 American League Championship Series. He observed Cal Ripken Jr.'s stance in the back corner of the batter's box. From this position, Hoyt knew Ripken wanted an inside low fastball. True to his theory of feeding the hitter what he doesn't want to see, Hoyt "just beat the hell out of the outside corner with fastballs, and [Ripken] never swung at them."

During a different game with a two-run lead and some wiggle room, Hoyt tested his theory. He threw Ripken the pitch he wanted.

"I threw him a low inside fastball, and he tattooed it. Bounced it into left center. One-hopped the left center-field fence. Good thing it didn't go out."

If Hoyt had a lead and he wouldn't lose it with a home run, he experimented. "I'll just go ahead and throw them what I think they're looking for just to make sure they're looking for it. That might help me further down the line."

Former teammate Britt Burns always wondered why Hoyt gave up so many home runs. Years later, upon hearing Hoyt's reasoning of testing the waters of throwing a pitch he thought the batter wanted, Burns was floored. "So that's what you were doing?" he asked.

"That's all."

Some hitters were easier to gauge than others. Hoyt singles out Wade Boggs. "He had the best eye. You miss the plate by a quarter of an inch, he took it as a ball. If it caught any of the plate at all, he'd foul it off. And then he'd get you in a situation where you had to get the ball over a lot of the plate, and that's how he got so many hits."

## BEGINNINGS

Hoyt grew up in Columbia, South Carolina. He maintains that the city's heat and humidity make it an ideal location for players to develop endurance to play baseball in the hot summer.

He started playing baseball as a boy by throwing a ball against a brick wall at his mother's house. "I had a little square of black electrical tape I used to put up on the wall for what was the strike zone. And I would try and hit the inside corner, the outside corner." Hoyt believes this initial work helped develop his control. It also honed his defense. "The ball's going to come back to you faster than when you throw it. So when you finish, you have to be in a good position to catch it."

Hoyt was eight years old when his Little League manager asked him to pitch. Knowing his son was going to the mound, his father, Dewey, called LaMarr over to the sidelines.

"Let me show you something," Dewey said to his son. He demonstrated a slider grip of keeping the pointer and middle fingers together and placing them across the seams of the ball. "Throw it just like a fastball, but this'll make the ball move a little bit. Take some speed off of it. Think you got it?"

The son nodded yes to his father.

"I'm not going to let you go out there and throw your fastball over and get your head bashed in. I'm going to give you something off-speed you can throw them off kilter with."

The boy took the mound and pitched well. Learning the slider from his father, Hoyt used the pitch his entire career in the major leagues.

Attending Keenan High School, Hoyt was an all-around athlete. In addition to baseball, he played basketball and football. As a football player, he had multiple talents: He quarterbacked, played middle line-backer, and punted. He remembers one game when time was winding down and Keenan held a slim lead and little production on offense. Deep on Keenan's side of the field, Hoyt's coach asked him to kick the ball as far as he could.

"I kicked the ball 80 yards," Hoyt says. "It sailed over the punt returner's head. He didn't even move. He just looked up at it and watched it land in the end zone."

His strong leg and arm attracted the interest of colleges offering football scholarships.

"Nearly every school in the Southeast wanted me: Georgia, Georgia Tech, North Carolina, Carson-Newman, Clemson."

Hoyt also received multiple baseball scholarship offers. Surprisingly, though, the hometown University of South Carolina Gamecocks showed no interest in him.

"Bobby Richardson watched me pitch one time. He was the coach at USC. My dad went over to him and said, 'Well, what do you think, Coach?' Richardson just said, 'He's not college material.' Later on, I found out that Richardson wrote a letter to the New York Yankees and told them to keep an eye on me, but I never heard a word from USC."

After his senior year in high school in 1973, Hoyt was weighing his opportunities when the New York Yankees drafted him in the fifth round. He signed, became a professional baseball player, and reported to rookie ball in Johnson City, Tennessee. He spent the next seven seasons in the minor leagues. He liked how the Yankees treated their players ("Like gold," Hoyt says) and how they brought legends like Joe DiMaggio, Mickey Mantle, and Whitey Ford to spend time around the team during spring training. One preseason, Hoyt learned many lessons from future Hall of Famer and 1974 American League Cy Young Award winner Jim "Catfish" Hunter.

"Billy Martin got ticked off at me one spring training and told me he was going to put me on the Catfish Hunter program." Shadowing Hunter's every move, Hoyt quickly learned that this meant working harder than anyone else in camp. "If everybody else ran 20 poles, Catfish ran 40. And, he's always looking over his shoulder: 'Are you keeping up, kid?'"

A control pitcher, Hoyt was amazed to hear Hunter tell him that Hoyt's pitches were the same that Hunter threw. "He was one of the really nice guys in baseball. His head didn't get larger because of his accomplishments," Hoyt says.

Approachable, Hunter spent time with Hoyt during batting practice, explaining how he made the ball move and then asking Hoyt, "Is there anything else you want to know? What else can I tell you?"

Before Hoyt could make it to the big leagues as a Yankee, the team included him in a trade with the Chicago White Sox in April 1977 for shortstop Bucky Dent. If the Yankees treated their players like gold, the White Sox treated theirs more like stone.

"When Bill Veeck owned the team, it was one of the poorest organizations in baseball. Had trouble meeting payroll every other week," Hoyt says. The lack of cash flow meant that minor-league players doubled as groundskeepers. "We had to maintain the field ourselves. But we learned tricks. When we built the mound for the visitor's bullpen, we would make it a little cockeyed. Turned a little off-center so you're throwing back across your body. And then, you get out there on the real mound, you're throwing straight at the strike zone."

Although regarded as one of the top pitchers in the Yankees' farm system, Hoyt felt overlooked in the White Sox minor leagues. So committed to making it to the big leagues, he began pitching nearly year-round, spending a season in the minors, then going to the winter leagues in the Dominican Republic, then reporting to spring training and starting the cycle again.

"I just wanted an organization to notice me," Hoyt says. "I had been in the minor leagues for seven years."

Winter ball was Hoyt's first time to play with LaRussa. Hoyt spent a lot of time with his manager.

"He had the apartment right below me. And the good thing about it was, we would sit down at the beach every day and talk about things."

LaRussa saw Hoyt's talent, and he told the pitcher that to improve his chances of making it to the major leagues, he needed to be versatile. As a result, Hoyt mixed his appearances. He would start a game on Sunday afternoon, then pitch some short and long relief during the week, and then be ready to start a game the following Sunday.

Hoyt's approach helped him accomplish his goal. By 1979, he arrived in the major leagues. As a 59-year-old man in 2014 looking back on his career, he questions whether the year-round cycle of pitching led to his shoulder injuries and being out of baseball and retired by the time he was 31. But on September 14, 1979, after stops in Johnson City, Fort Lauderdale, West Haven, Iowa, Knoxville, Appleton, and the winter leagues, he finally arrived. He stepped on Comiskey Park's mound in the ninth inning and made his major-league debut against the Oakland A's.

"I turned around and looked up and thought about my mother and thought, 'Well, if this is what you're going to do for a living, make this the best damn pitch you ever threw.'"

With that, Hoyt read the catcher's signs and threw a pitch to Rickey Henderson. Hoyt retired him and the next hitter with fly balls, and the third hitter tapped a groundball to shortstop for an easy out. Three up and three down.

Despite the success, Hoyt started the 1980 season in Triple-A Iowa. The White Sox promoted him in June, and, consistent with his beach conversations with LaRussa in winter ball years earlier, Hoyt played different roles on the staff, pitching in relief and stepping in and handling some starts. He discovered some preferences—he liked using Wilson gloves ("I wanted it to be firm. When I reached out to catch balls, the ball needs to stick in the glove."), Adidas shoes (similar to gloves, Hoyt wanted new, firm shoes), and pitching from the mound in Oakland–Alameda County Coliseum. ("The mound seems to be a little bit higher. The park's a little bigger—it's just conducive for pitchers.") He pitched well, winning nine games in both 1980 and 1981, and by the end of April 1982, he found himself in the starting rotation, winning 19 games and throwing 11 complete games, including two shutouts.

"When I was out there, I wanted to leave everything I had on the field," Hoyt says. "I wanted to finish the game."

Hoyt says he could concentrate and have tunnel vision to examine what part of the plate the hitter was giving him. Take it. Get ahead in the count. Then, depending on the score, the inning, the situation, determine what to throw. He compares it to a golfer being in the zone and dissecting the different elements—the distance, the wind, the hazards—and having perfect concentration to make the correct decisions. This may be Hoyt's natural makeup. But he also notes that the White Sox hired a hypnotist to help players concentrate. "It was mandatory. Everybody had to see him. He wore this ring that had a dinky stone in it, and you had to look at the stone while he gave you positive thoughts. Like 'You're on the mound. Nothing else matters. There's no negativity. You're ultrasuccessful.'"

## CONDITIONING

Traditionally, pitching coaches run pitchers. The philosophy is that with a strong lower body, the pitcher will have power pushing off the rubber and endurance to pitch deep into games.

Hoyt hated running.

"I just didn't like to run," he says. "It messes with your knees and your back, and I wanted to avoid shin splints and all of that."

In spring training, White Sox pitching coach Dave Duncan sent pitchers on a two-mile loop outside the stadium for their conditioning. Hoyt discovered a shortcut and a shady porch near the finish where he waited for the other runners.

"I'd cut off over there, talk with the guy for a little bit. Those players would run by, and I'd say, 'I got to go.' And I'd fall right in line behind them. I'd be sweating like the rest of them. 'Man, that was hell this morning, running that two-mile run.'"

Rumors spread that Hoyt left the rest of the running pitchers to duck into a bar and drink beer, but he dismisses this story.

"It's not even realistic," he says. "Hell, they weren't open at eight o'clock in the morning. It's kind of funny the way rumors get started and get blown around. I've had my share of them, good and bad."

Hoyt talked with White Sox trainer Herm Schneider to find an alternative to running, and Schneider introduced him to biking, an activity Hoyt loved.

"I'd ride the bicycle for 20 minutes, doing intervals. Warm up for three minutes, doing whatever speed you want. Then go as fast as you can go. And repeat."

In the offseason, Hoyt pedaled the streets of his Columbia neighborhood, and he says the workouts left him in great shape. And they were fun. Later in his career, Hoyt and teammate Goose Gossage hopped on stationary bicycles and blasted country music and pedaled hard. "We used to get the clubhouse rocking, and we're in there riding our bikes like hell, sweating our asses off. Me and Goose used to have a good time."

After Schneider placed him on a biking regimen, Hoyt would sit in a lawn chair on the outfield grass and heckle pitchers as they ran. "I'd be telling them to pick up the pace. Run harder," he says with a laugh. "But, I loved riding a bike. I rode every day."

Hoyt also used an elbow flexing machine, a hydraulic stirrup-like device designed for tennis players to avoid tennis elbow. Hoyt used it to build arm strength, and he found that it helped him throw breaking balls.

During the season, Hoyt also prepared through bullpen sessions.

"I just warmed up a little bit," he says. "I never counted pitches or anything like that. I'd make sure that I had my fastballs down, my cut fastballs down, my curveballs down, and my changeups down, and once I was satisfied with each one in my repertoire, I'd be happy and walk off."

Hoyt also believes in the value of rest so the body can recover and rejuvenate. He liked to throw complete games (of his 172 career starts, he finished 48), and he didn't want to wear himself out by running every day.

His ability to throw so many complete games earned him the nickname "Horse"—Hoyt would carry a heavy load just like a workhorse.

He also listened to his pitching coaches, especially Dave Duncan.

"He didn't force anything on you," Hoyt says. "He just laid out the percentages and made it real clear that, when you get ahead in the count, your chances of getting the hitter out go way up. You're going to win 70 percent of your games. Simple. Works simple. If you give up hits at even counts, you'll be a .500 pitcher. Give up hits behind in the count, you'll win 20 percent of your games. He drilled that into me: the importance of getting ahead in the count."

A student of the game, Hoyt applied the various lessons—the tips from Catfish Hunter, the aerodynamics from Michael Rusk, the importance of getting ahead in the count—and developed his own views on pitching.

"I know the strike zone's supposed to be a square. But I look at it as a circle, and it has lights on it. And I could throw fastballs right down the middle and move them and knock out any light you want anytime."


## EXPECTATIONS

Hoyt entered the 1983 season with high expectations, but the season started slowly. By mid-May, his record was two wins and six losses, and his earned-run average climbed over 5. But after the All-Star break, Hoyt was unbeatable: he won 12 games and lost none. True to his nickname, six of these games were complete games, one of which was a shutout and another of which Hoyt pitched 10 innings.

Hoyt found a routine that worked well for him. On days he pitched, he liked to arrive at the ballpark shortly before game time. He stepped into the training room where the trainer rubbed his right arm with baby oil to loosen it. He took two ibuprofen tablets and drank two cups of coffee.

"Black coffees," he says.

Then he would step outside to pitch.

In 1983, Hoyt's routine worked well as he posted 23 wins, most in the American League.

Although Hall of Fame catcher Carlton Fisk was his teammate who caught the majority of Hoyt's 36 starts, Hoyt preferred Marc Hill, whom Hoyt calls "Booter" (as in Boot Hill), as his batterymate.

"[Fisk] is a great catcher, but he did things that irritated me," Hoyt says. "He'd take too long in between pitches. I was one of these guys who wanted to get on the rubber and throw it immediately. I wanted to set the pace of the game."

Reminded of his pitching rhythm, Hoyt laughs. "I wanted to get in and off the mound as fast as possible. They used to say that I pitched like I was double parked."

The yin to his yang, Fisk slowed the pace.

"He'd stand up, bullshit with the hitter. He'd fix his mask, fix his cup, fix his pants. Then get down in his crouch. And then is ready to go. And I'm like, 'Man, I've been ready to throw the ball 10 minutes ago. What are you doing?'"

In contrast, Booter followed Hoyt's lead and set up behind the plate quickly. Hoyt admits that at times he could work too fast and that Fisk was good about slowing things down. But another thing that drew Hoyt to Hill was Booter's pitch selection. "The catcher makes a suggestion for the pitch," Hoyt says. "I'd shake Carlton off because his pitch selections were obvious. He may as well tell the guy what's coming. First pitch: fastball inside. Do that and go pick it up 400 feet away 'cause that's where it's going to be." Hill, though, didn't telegraph to the hitters what Hoyt and he were doing.

In addition to thinking alike about pitch selection, Hoyt and Booter shared a physical resemblance—similar frames (both men are 6-foot-3 and weighed around 200 pounds), brown hair and beards. The two were often mistaken for each other, so much so that Hill could pose as Hoyt and sign autographs as the pitcher.

When Hoyt won the Cy Young Award, the White Sox won 99 games and the American League West Division, boasting an enviable combination of hitting and pitching. Greg Luzinski and Ron Kittle provided power with 32 and 35 home runs, respectively. Hoyt's fellow starting pitchers Floyd Bannister and Richard Dotson also posted spectacular seasons, winning 16 and 22 games, respectively. In Hoyt's mind, Dotson could have won the Cy Young Award just as easily given his pitching dominance in 1983.

"He had a much better ERA," Hoyt says. "Lost only two games in the second half of the season—both of them were home runs in the bottom of the ninth inning."

While these factors contributed to the team's success, Hoyt points to a midseason trade with the Seattle Mariners that brought second baseman Julio Cruz to the South Side of Chicago as a key for the team's success.

"That guy had some ungodly range," Hoyt says. "And to bring him in to a pitching staff that just did nothing but have guys hit the ball on the ground? I mean, he caught everything."

Another key contributor was Dennis Lamp, a versatile pitcher who started five games for the White Sox, saved 15, and pitched 116 1/3 innings.

"Dennis Lamp was a very important factor of our pitching staff because he could do long relief, short relief, intermediate starts, and do it well." Hoyt recalls Lamp having an 11–0 record for Toronto a few years later and wishes these wins had been for the White Sox instead of the Blue Jays.

Lamp also kept the clubhouse loose.

"He could mimic anything," Hoyt says. "He'd get guys to laugh and relax. That's the way you have to be to play baseball. You have to relax. Especially if you're pitching. Take a deep breath. Let it out. Then get lined up. Don't hold your breath. Don't tense up because if you tense anything up, you're just going to take velocity off the ball."

For Hoyt, a key moment in the season was disposing of the Kansas City Royals, seemingly a perennial playoff team that always finished ahead of Chicago.

"We had a September homestand against the Kansas City Royals," Hoyt says. "Historically, we'd fade, and the Royals would move past us. But I told the reporters this time it was going to be different. 'They won't beat me, Floyd, and Richard.' I said it before I did it, and I had to back it up."

Hoyt backed it up by pitching a four-hit shutout on September 1. When he pitched, he blocked out distractions and focused on the hitter and working with the catcher. But during this game against the Royals in the eighth inning, he felt vibrations, and he realized that Comiskey Park was chanting in unison, "La-Marr! La-Marr! La-Marr!"

Hoyt's skin prickled from the praise. He stepped off the rubber and walked to the back of the mound. He picked up the rosin bag.

"I was like, 'My God. We're getting it done.'"

He enjoyed the moment; then he threw the rosin bag down and finished the game.

He also finished the game in the American League Championship Series against the Baltimore Orioles. Hoyt made one postseason appearance in his career, and he made the most of it, starting and completing game one of the Championship Series at Memorial Stadium. Earning the win, he gave up only one run and only five hits as the White Sox won 2–1.

As Hoyt took the mound to pitch that postseason game in Baltimore following a rain delay, a rainbow appeared over Memorial Stadium. Hoyt says people have brought up the rainbow to him, that it was a fitting sign for a pitcher who had a spectacular season and who was preparing to pitch another excellent game. Hoyt doesn't remember the rainbow or a sign of symbolism overhead. He recalls walking up and down the runway between the dugout and the clubhouse, drinking black coffee, focused and in the zone.

"There was no way I could have lost that day," Hoyt said.[3]

Though Hoyt ended the season on a high note, the White Sox did not. Chicago lost the next three games to the Orioles, and Baltimore advanced to the World Series. With the White Sox' year ended, they had to take solace in winning their first division title since 1959.

"If the series had gone to a fifth game, there's no way we would have lost that series, either," Hoyt said, confident in his ability to have kept the White Sox postseason hopes alive.[4]


## AFTER THE CY

Hoyt spent one more season in the South Side of Chicago then headed west to San Diego as part of a trade—Ozzie Guillen, Tim Lollar, Bill Long, and Luis Salazar became White Sox; in exchange, Hoyt became a Padre. Hoyt pitched great in the National League in 1985, winning 16 games, posting a 3.47 ERA, throwing three shutouts, and starting the All-Star Game and earning Most Valuable Player honors in the mid-summer classic. But an injury to his shoulder derailed his career, as did arrests for drugs. Hoyt spent time in prison in the late 1980s on drug-related charges. After his release, he returned to his hometown, Columbia, South Carolina, and began a career in sales. In 2014, he was teaching pitching lessons, and he had reconnected with the White Sox, sharing lessons learned 25 years earlier with the next generation of pitchers.

"I enjoy talking to kids about baseball," Hoyt says. "I'm happy to share that knowledge with them. Baseball has been good to me. Being a starting pitcher is the best job in the world: pitch every fifth day, play a great game, and get paid a lot of money. I was given a gift, and I need to share it and teach it."

When teaching, Hoyt is flexible. He doesn't believe there's only way to pitch. "I don't mess with anybody's natural delivery. I just want to make sure they have good fundamentals. Don't stress your body."

He also holds out hope that a minor-league team will return to Columbia and that he can share some of his experiences as a pitching coach.

"I told Jerry Reinsdorf that he needs to bring a minor-league team to Columbia. I'd be his pitching coach. With what I know about pitching and Richard Dotson showing them that changeup in Triple-A Charlotte, there's no telling how good the White Sox would be."

# 6

# SETTLED IN: DENNIS ECKERSLEY

## 1992 AMERICAN LEAGUE CY YOUNG AWARD

*Dennis Eckersley and I began our conversation by talking about catchers. First up: Charlie O'Brien, who, over the course of 15 years in the big leagues, caught 13 Cy Young Award winners.*

*"I know Charlie," Eckersley said. "He was a good catcher. Going back to my days, I think he was with Milwaukee—is that accurate?"*

*Later on, Eckersley brought up working with Ron Hassey and Jamie Quirk while in Oakland and the targets they presented. "Jamie had a small, little target. He'd get real small somehow. And Hassey was a big, spread-out catcher," Eckersley said. "I liked Hassey. He could sort of get that corner. He would spread out, and you didn't know he was out there about six inches. But Jamie would sort of pinch it."*

*Talk of targets reminded Eckersley of his early days in Boston and working with Carlton Fisk.*

*"Big, tall," Eckersley said. "He was great [at being a target]. The problem with Fisk: It was his tempo. You know, how he was so fucking slow. He drove me crazy because I was like, ready. It probably helped me. Of course, I'm complaining about it now, 35 years later, but he probably slowed me down. It probably helped me. I needed to slow down because I was probably going too fast. But it drove me nuts, somebody trying to lasso you. God, he used to take a long time just to even get set. And then he'd come out and take his mask off and come out to the mound. Like, God! But, he was a great catcher. He was the best I ever had."*

*Eckersley worked with a lot of catchers. After all, he played for 24 seasons and pitched in 1,071 games, fifth most all-time. Eckersley has a multitude of baseball experiences to reflect on, but we focused on 1992 when he was named the American League's best pitcher as well as its Most Valuable Player. He was surprised by the MVP honors, and, in fact, he said pitchers shouldn't win the MVP.*

*"I know there's been some incredible years," he said. "Not mine in particular . . . I don't know. It's hard to put the importance of 200-something innings. Mine was different. Mine was nothing. Mine came down to a matter of there was nobody that was clear cut, so the vote gets spread out. That's how that happened. Nobody had this great offensive year."*

*Voters, however, disagreed.*

In 1992, a familiar scene ended Oakland A's wins: Dennis Eckersley emerging from the bullpen for the top of the ninth inning. As George Thorogood's "Bad to the Bone" blared through Oakland–Alameda County Coliseum's speakers, Eckersley stepped across the left-field grass, long, dark hair poking from his cap, his face stern. Once he reached the mound, manager Tony LaRussa handed him the ball, patted him on the ass, and told him to go get 'em.

Eckersley nodded. He waited for his catcher, usually Jamie Quirk as a ninth-inning defensive replacement, to return to home plate. Then he warmed up, rocking back into his windup, uncorking fastballs and sliders, his delivery three-quarters and low, dipping toward third base in a big swing as he released the ball. ("I needed time to unfold," Eckersley says, referring to his motion.)[1]

And then, it was time to notch the last three outs of the game, a role he had been fulfilling with distinction for five seasons, leading the American League in saves in 1988 and becoming in 1990 only the second pitcher in baseball history to post an earned-run average less than 1 for a season.[2]

As he prepared to face the hitter, Eckersley focused on the catcher's mitt. His face projected intensity. Yet internally, emotions roiled.

"People think you're so cool out there. Bullshit," Eckersley says. "You're uptight. To me, every game was like life or death. Seriously, I could get geared up to the point of having an upset stomach."

He masked the anxiety with swagger like the growling guitar chords on the public address system.

"My whole thing was I didn't want anybody to know what was going on inside," he says. "It's all about body language. You can't let them know. But, to be honest with you, inside, I was grinding all the time."

As a veteran in his 18th major-league season, Eckersley could harness the adrenaline to focus on executing his pitches.

"A lot of guys, you could shit all over yourself with that [pressure]. But, for me, it fine-tuned my focus. You're so channeled. But I had been around so long. I mean, I wasn't a kid. It made me better than I was. As good as I could be, that ninth inning."

Eckersley liked for his first pitch to be a breaking ball for strike one. As he began his delivery, he closed his left eye, almost as if he were wincing or aiming down a sight, and fired.

"I just went after people," he says. "I think if you throw strike one with a breaking ball and the hitter hasn't seen you, you've got him. Now, he hasn't seen your fastball. You can throw your breaking ball different speeds, and he's vulnerable to your fastball in. It sets up the whole count. If I threw strike one to a hitter with a breaking ball, I felt like I was in total control."

His pitching style has been described as aggressive, which Eckersley believes means confronting hitters. "It's just trying to get ahead. . . . That's basically what pitching's about," he says.

At 37 years old, Eckersley didn't have the same speed he had years earlier to blast fastballs and overpower hitters. ("You can't act like fucking Goose Gossage when you ain't got that kind of gas," he says.) Instead, he relied on excellent control, a 91-mph fastball he could paint the black with, and his slider, a pitch he learned early in his career from Dick Tidrow. With his slider, Eckersley could throw it hard, soft, and softer, and he says having the ability to throw it different speeds is the secret to a good slider.

When he achieved the result he wanted and recorded the final three outs, he released the tension and displayed his emotions, pumping his fists or yelling.

"That was just letting out all of that anxiety," Eckersley says. "People don't know that. They think you're trying to show somebody up. For Christ's sake, I was never premeditated. If I pointed at the catcher

**Dennis Eckersley: Aim . . . Courtesy of the National Baseball Hall of Fame and Museum, Cooperstown, N.Y.**

**Dennis Eckersley: . . . fire. Courtesy of the National Baseball Hall of Fame and Museum, Cooperstown, N.Y.**

when you called the last strike, like 'That's a strike! Call it!' it was just, get him out of here!"

Eckersley's goal was to have a short outing—get in, get the job done in 15 pitches or less, and get out.

"At that age, you can't be throwing a lot of pitches."

## STARTING TO RELIEVING

Eckersley discovered closing midway through his career after spending 12 years in the big leagues as a starter. Eckersley was incredibly effective as a starting pitcher, winning 20 games in 1978, finishing in the Top 10 for wins twice (1978 and 1979), and, on May 30, 1977, pitching a no-hitter for the Cleveland Indians.

"I was so young," he says. "Back in those days, I was trying to throw a no-no every time I used to pitch. I'd get pissed the first hit. I can't believe I used to think like that, but that's how I was."

Even though nearly 40 years have passed since Memorial Day 1977, Eckersley still recalls the no-hitter's last out.

"I think [the last batter] was Gil Flores. I punched him out. And there were no cameras there. We weren't even on TV for Christ's sake. Getting the last out, I was yelling at him because he wouldn't get in the box."

Flores delayed as cameramen scurried into foul territory to set up their tripods to capture an image of the no-hitter's last out. Eckersley didn't cotton to the stalling.

"Hey!" Eckersley screamed at Flores. "They're not here to take your picture! You're the last out. Get your fucking ass in there!"

In hindsight, Eckersley reflects, "That's the crazy shit I used to do. But that's who I was. I mean, I was somebody else, looking back now."

Indeed, in 1987, his life and career were at a crossroads. His fastball had slowed. And, after seeing a video of himself inebriated at his daughter's birthday party, he decided to seek treatment for alcoholism.

"When I went into rehab 35 years ago, 30 years ago, whatever it was, it was sort of hush-hush," he says. "Now, it's like no big deal, right? Who *hasn't* gone into recovery? Goddamn. Which is not such a bad thing because you'll get some help. It's a big part of my story. Because I wouldn't have got there without it. It wouldn't have happened."

Fresh from rehabilitation, Eckersley was in spring training with the Chicago Cubs, just trying to get back on track and get his work in. Facing the Oakland A's, Eckersley was getting hammered, giving up six runs in two innings. Then slugger Jose Canseco added to the hit total, clubbing a double off the outfield wall.

Eckersley put the hit behind him and focused on the next pitch when Canseco broke from second base to steal third.

"I'm like, what?" Eckersley says. "It's spring training. It's 6–0."

Eckersley glared at Canseco, and Canseco shrugged.

"Don't look at me," Canseco said, and he pointed to the dugout.

Eckersley stared into the dugout, and he saw LaRussa.

"Yeah!" LaRussa said. "It's me! I told him to go."

"Well, fuck you!" Eckersley roared.

Two weeks later, the Cubs traded Eckersley. To the A's. And another transition. After a career of starting, Eckersley shifted to the bullpen.

"It couldn't have come at a better time," he says. "I was so together, physically and emotionally, everything. It was like a new life. I mean, I was excited about being ready to play every day. After starting for so many years like that, just being ready every five days, there's nights you come to the ballpark, you're not going to play. It's like you're just a cheerleader. But, I'm telling you, as a reliever, you're like an everyday player. You may not pitch, but you are geared up to pitch! It's exhausting. But you're alive every day. So it couldn't have come at a better time for me. I was so hungry to prove myself again. I mean, it's incredible. You get the opportunity. It all just came together. Tony LaRussa, here we go."

## DYNASTY

In the late 1980s, the Oakland A's emerged as the American League's—if not Major League Baseball's—premier team, winning three consecutive pennants beginning in 1988 and winning the 1989 World Series. Jose Canseco became the game's first player to hit 40 home runs and steal 40 bases in the same season and won Most Valuable Player honors in 1988. Mark McGwire set the record for most home runs in a season by a rookie (49) in 1987. Bob Welch won 27 games, the most wins in a season since 1972, en route to the 1990 American League Cy Young Award. Fitting perfectly within this context, Eckersley emerged as the game's elite closer, compiling 185 saves from 1987 through 1991. And, in one sense, the 1992 Oakland A's continued the dominating trend, winning 96 games and the American League Western Division.

Eckersley agrees. "We felt like we would win it every year."

But he also says his Cy Young and Most Valuable Player season was the last hurrah for the A's dynasty.

"They were going to break it up," he says. "Moneywise, they couldn't do it anymore."

Although the A's won nearly two-thirds of their games, the team did so despite multiple injuries. Outfielders Dave Henderson, Canseco, and Hall of Famer Rickey Henderson all spent time on the disabled list, but LaRussa mixed and matched, using 59 different lineups to produce wins. McGwire had an exceptional year, blasting 42 home runs, but two players from the season stand out to Eckersley. One is Carney Lansford, who missed the 1991 season due to injuries and who announced 1992 would be his final year as a player.

"He was our captain," Eckersley says. "[Carney] was a grinder, man. He was intense. The chemistry is based on that, the guys like that that play hard every day."

The other teammate who comes to mind is Jerry Browne.

"The Governor, right?" Eckersley laughs. "He was perfect because he played a lot of different positions. You need that guy."

In terms of role players, LaRussa used this concept in the bullpen as well. Unlike managers who wait to bring in a relief pitcher to get out of jams, LaRussa methodically presented middle relievers and his closer with a clean slate at the top of an inning with no baserunners and no outs. The usual sequence at the end of the game: Gene Nelson, Rick Honeycutt, and then Eckersley.

"Honeycutt was so important to me. Because he would get that left-hander. He'd get that tough left-hander. If he didn't, it's a domino effect." He pauses. "Honeycutt, I couldn't have done what I did all those years without Honeycutt."

The precise role benefited Eckersley. And LaRussa placed him in situations where he would succeed.

"It's just all good situations," he says. "If I did give up a run, I had two or three [as a lead]. Because, if you have a year, say, you give up 10 or 12 runs a year. That's a good year. But you've given up 12 saves if you only have a one-run lead!"

Put another way, a relief pitcher needs room to make a mistake. LaRussa recognized that. He also used Eckersley judiciously.

"Think about it," Eckersley says. "At my age, if he didn't use me the right way, he could have burned me out. Or I just wouldn't have been successful or helped him or the team."

To that end, Eckersley pitched 80 innings.

"I wouldn't say [I was] pampered but taken care of. Watched over as well as you can."

With everyone having clear roles, the bullpen maintained a business-like atmosphere. No hijinks.

"We didn't fart around like clowns. You hear stories about bullpens and stuff, but the problem is, by the time I get there, everybody else is done. So they're off the hook. The pressure's on me. And I can't stand sitting next to somebody who doesn't have any type pressure that I have, and they're farting around."

The team rocked along, spending most of the season in first place and Eckersley cruising, including a game on April 20 when he struck out five consecutive California Angels. Then general manager Sandy Alderson made a blockbuster trade, sending Jose Canseco to division rival Texas for outfielder Ruben Sierra, starting pitcher Bobby Witt, and relief pitcher Jeff Russell.

"Jose was shocked," Eckersley says. "The look on his face. He couldn't believe they had traded him."

Eckersley says the trade was a good one, not in terms of pushing the A's over the hump to make the playoffs, but by bringing in three solid, steady contributors to the team.

"It really shook up the club," he says. "There's no doubt about it. . . . It was the right thing to do. Because Jose was a pain in the ass. He just was."

Eckersley explains Canseco felt like he received less favorable treatment from the press than teammate McGwire, similar to an inferiority complex. Canseco could create a distraction, but Eckersley learned to block him out. But now that he would be a member of the Rangers, Canseco's distractions would be in Arlington, not Oakland.

The A's main competition in 1992 was the Minnesota Twins, winners of the 1991 World Series. A big moment for Eckersley and the A's was going into the Hubert H. Humphrey Metrodome and sweeping the Twins late in the season. Eric Fox, a rookie outfielder who appeared in 51 games that season, was an unlikely hero for Oakland in that series, launching a Rick Aguilera pitch over the right-field fence for a three-run home run. The timing was dramatic: When Fox began the at-bat, it was the top of the ninth inning with the A's trailing 2–4.

"When that ball went out of the ballpark, everybody shit their pants because this kid just took him deep. Now everybody's jumping up and down," Eckersley says.

Although teammates were happy, Eckersley was subdued.

"I had to pitch. Hello! I had to hurry up and get ready. That's why I remember that game. Trying to get ready quickly and everybody's excited, and I've got to close this thing down. I'm like, 'Calm down.'"

The team played well at its home field, Oakland–Alameda County Coliseum, winning 51 of 81 games. Eckersley loved pitching at home.

"Wish I would have started there," he says. "Because I was a fly-ball pitcher even though I was a sinkerball guy. When I used to start, I would give up some bombs because I was always around the plate. I lived with it. O.co was a good place to pitch. Oakland was my favorite."

(His least favorite park to pitch in? Wrigley Field. "Wrigley Field was no pleasure," he says with a laugh. "Especially Wrigley Field in the summer. Are you kidding me? I'd be taking BP, and I'd be going bridge. I'd be going deep. We're in trouble.")

Eckersley achieved considerable success in 1992, saving 40 consecutive games from the beginning of the season through August 23.

"I just recall everything falling into place for me," he says. "I couldn't do anything wrong. Even when I did something wrong, somebody caught it. It's just everything going your way. Every time you go into a game, I'd get the save."

Although the success was frequent, he maintained an even keel. "The highs didn't last very long. You're shaking hands [after the game], and it's like, oh, God, we've got to do this again. You couldn't get too carried away."

The bottom line: Eckersley was performing at an optimal level.

"At that point in my career, that was my peak physically. I think complete control of your body and your mind. You're just at a level as high as you can go. And not having to be necessarily durable. It's just a 15-pitch act. That's it. But you couldn't find a guy better prepared for it.

Physically. Mentally. I was just peaking. I had been doing it for like five years. Man, we were like a machine. It was beautiful."

The season ended for Eckersley and the A's in the American League Championship Series, with the Toronto Blue Jays, not the A's, advancing to the World Series. After a long season, Eckersley's elbow was sore. And he was tired.

"I wasn't throwing so good. I kind of ran out of gas. Of all times, you know?"

He also heard whispers that the Blue Jays detected which pitches he was going to throw, so he started throwing from the stretch even with no baserunners. Eckersley made three postseason appearances that year, but the one that stands out is not a moment he savors, a home run to Roberto Alomar in Game Four, an afternoon game at Oakland. In the top of the ninth inning with the A's leading 6–4 and with one baserunner on, Alomar tied the game by taking Eckersley deep. The Blue Jays eventually won in 11 innings.

"The Alomar home run crushed me," he says. "I felt so responsible for that season. That game got away from us, and Alomar got me, and we ended up losing to the Blue Jays, and I was crushed. That had such a lingering effect on me. It affected all this good stuff that happened."

Comparing the Alomar home run with the often-replayed home run Kirk Gibson hit off Eckersley during the 1988 World Series, Eckersley says the Alomar home run hurt more.

"It was in my gut. That one brought me to my knees. You can't have it all. I almost had it all."

One month later, Eckersley was awarded the Cy Young and Most Valuable Player honors for the American League.

"I know it sounds corny, but I would have given them up," he says, thinking of the Championship Series and the other team advancing but the A's concluding their season.


## THE STEROID ERA

Two of Eckersley's teammates, Canseco and McGwire, have been primary subjects in the steroid era and the impact of performance-enhancing drugs in baseball. Canseco's book *Juiced* addresses his use of PEDs and implicates other players seeking a competitive edge. In 2005, both

Canseco and McGwire appeared before a congressional committee investigating steroids to testify about PEDs. Just seven years earlier in 1998, McGwire helped bring fans back to baseball as he chased and eclipsed Roger Maris's single-season home-run record. Although he retired with 583 home runs and 500 was previously a lock for Cooperstown, McGwire is not in the Hall of Fame.

Eckersley spent multiple seasons around bulked-up teammates. His clubhouse had blenders humming, mixing protein shakes, regularly. He says he was oblivious or naïve about steroid use.

"I was clueless," he says. "There's a lot of people who were clueless."

Eckersley says he was so focused on getting his job done that he didn't think about why teammates were so strong and muscle bound. He was running four miles a day, playing catch, eating a turkey sandwich for lunch, and adhering to the routine that brought him success instead of spending much time thinking about what teammates were doing.

"I never thought of it like, 'Oh, my God! Look at those guys. They're cheating, and guess what? We get to win because they are.' I wasn't even thinking like that. I was just thinking, 'Jesus Christ, these guys are lifting weights.' I sound like I'm clueless, but nobody knew what was going on, not even the press. You have to go back to the times and be there to understand. It's easy to look back now."

Eckersley takes a hard stance against PED users being in the Hall of Fame. That said, he understands it's a thorny issue.

"The problem is there's guys that didn't get caught," he says. "So, that means you hammer the guy that did or . . ." He pauses. "It's all a matter of you thought they did, almost, when it comes to the voting, right? I mean, I think it's a shame, but I don't think they should go in the Hall of Fame. I just don't. If you're going to start splitting hairs saying, 'I don't know how long a guy did it, he was a Hall of Famer before . . .' There's so many arguments."

## POSTPLAYING

Eckersley retired with 197 wins, 390 saves (seventh most all-time), 2,401 strikeouts, and a 3.50 ERA. In 2004, he was elected to the National Baseball Hall of Fame.

"The most incredible moment of my life is when the phone rang, and they say, 'You're in the Hall of Fame.' Ohh! That is a ridiculous moment. I can't even explain it. That was one of the most emotional moments of my life. It's like having a baby," he says with a laugh. "It's an unreal moment. Because you never think of yourself as that. Ever."

The euphoria was short lived as Eckersley soon learned that ESPN was working on a juicy story about him.

"It's like that took the fun out of it," he says. "They're coming whether you like it or not."

Eckersley focused on delivering his acceptance speech, an experience he likens to hearing one's eulogy. And a preoccupation during the Hall of Fame weekend.

"You wish you could have the speech, and then go. But the speech is at the end of the whole experience. So you're so uptight about the speech that you don't even have a good time before it! Right? That's me anyway. I always live in this sort of dread of having to perform. So that took away from it."

Once he delivered the speech, it was like clinching the save.

"Coming back after that, it was like, ahh. The heat's not on. Ultimately, it comes down to living in the moment. Enjoying the moment. It's hard for me. Because you feel like there's another game, you know? I've been talking about the past. You didn't necessarily live it when you go back. You wished sometimes you enjoyed the moments more."

Today, Eckersley divides his time between Boston and Florida. In the summers, he does some broadcasting work. He compares it to pitching.

"It's a double-edged sword, a mixed feeling. It's being live. It's like pitching. It's like the game's on the line. You hate to be nervous, but that's what it's all about because you're live. Literally. And it's something that's exhilarating, but it's as close as you can get to feeling that anxiousness, that adrenaline when you have to play."

In the winters, he plays "shitty golf."

"It's really hard being competitive and not being good at something. It's annoying."

And even though he retired from playing after the 1998 season, Eckersley still watches as much baseball as he can.

"I'm just this baseball guy," he says. "I watch every game. That's what I do. I've been doing it for a long time. Forty years."

Looking back, Eckersley is proud of his career and the way it shaped up. The timing was right.

"I couldn't imagine being in the bullpen, being 20 years old, throwing as hard as I did! I would have been inconsistently wild, probably."

"Blessed" is a word Eckersley uses.

"Twelve years of starting. Twelve years of relieving. The rehab in between the 12—are you kidding me? It was just a very blessed life."

He pauses, a man who just turned 60, his playing days nearly 20 years behind him.

"And I've got to figure it out from here on out."

# 7

# LABELS DON'T APPLY: JACK MCDOWELL

## 1993 AMERICAN LEAGUE CY YOUNG AWARD

*As we coordinated scheduling our interview, Jack McDowell asked, "What kind of beer do you drink?" My answer: whatever's cold. Then I asked him the same question, adding that, because he was agreeing to spend his Saturday evening with me, recounting his memories from 1993 when he was named the best pitcher in the American League and doing me the favor, I should provide the beer.*

*"Coors Light is my baby," he said.*

*Easy enough to remember as I stopped at the Harris Teeter grocery store by McDowell's neighborhood in Charlotte, North Carolina. I picked up some cold ones and made my way to McDowell's house. He opened the front door, and I immediately thought, "Man, he's tall." I knew he was tall from seeing him pitch on TV with the White Sox and Yankees and the statistics on the back of his baseball card: 6-foot-5. But in person, I was looking up to him.*

*We sat in his den, and three of his children, Molly, Rhett, and Rory, came in to say hello. I noticed a large square wooden frame on the wall holding at least a dozen LPs with predominantly blue covers: the Beatles' 1967–1970; Who's Next by the Who; the Replacements' first record. I like music, and I like discovering what other people are listening to. McDowell noticed I was staring at the collection of records, and he said, "Yeah, I made that a few years ago. I thought it'd be cool if I put all these old records together with blue covers. And there you have it."*

*We talked a little about music, how he enjoyed seeing the Replace-*
*ments live a long time ago and the Old 97s more recently in Asheville. I*
*wanted to ask more music questions, about what it was like being in a*
*band and participating in the music industry in the 1990s, his work*
*recognized in high-profile magazines like* Rolling Stone, *whether he*
*ever crossed paths with Alex Chilton or Paul Westerberg, all the while*
*toeing the mound as one of the league's best pitchers, but I didn't want*
*to take up too much of his time. That said, Jack McDowell is approach-*
*able and makes you feel comfortable, like you can crack open a Coors*
*Light and ask him a question about anything, and you know he's going*
*to answer you thoughtfully and directly, regardless of if the topic is*
*about music or baseball or rearing kids or neighborhoods in Charlotte.*

Although an elite pitcher who had just won 20 games in 1992, Jack
McDowell wanted more. His Chicago White Sox had finished third in
the American League Western Division[1], and after multiple seasons of
falling short to the Oakland A's, he was ready for his team to take the
next step and win the division.

"I was psycho about winning," McDowell says.[2]

To McDowell's credit, his team had a nucleus of talent that made his
expectation reasonable.

"Look at White Sox history, and the four straight number one picks,"
McDowell says. "It was me, Robin [Ventura], Frank [Thomas], and Alex
[Fernandez]. There you go. Out of four straight number one picks, you
have your Gold Glove leader third baseman, your MVP, your Cy Young
Award winner, and a legitimate number two starter. That's a ridiculous
accomplishment by [White Sox general manager] Larry Himes. And
yeah, you had to have everything else to put it together, but there's your
core that you can build off of."

On top of that, the White Sox had steady players like Ozzie Guillen
who could be counted on to be in the lineup nearly every day, play
smart, and pick up timely hits.

"You can have your superstars and this and that, but unless you have
guys you can pencil in, you can't build around that," McDowell says.
"You've got to have a guy in a season who's going to catch everything,
he's going to hit .270, and there he is. And now, if these [superstar] guys
have their years, we're going to win."

Knowing that, McDowell spent the offseason after 1992 in Chicago. To prepare his body for the grind of the upcoming year and to keep his arm in shape, he walked to a church in his neighborhood. Before leaving his house, he picked up a brand-new baseball and his glove. Some mornings were crisp and sunny, others dreary with snow flecking McDowell's goatee. Regardless, nearly every day, McDowell was outside the church, a solitary figure facing a brick wall. From 40 feet away, he started firing the pristine baseball into it.

"My whole idea was, it wasn't about pitching and command. It was about getting my arm strong enough to deal with everything," McDowell says. "I used to throw between 150 to 200 throws against the wall. As hard as I could. Threw against the wall and field the groundball. So, I'd field 200 groundballs, which is like 200 pickups in a training sense. Every one of them was fielding and throwing, so every one wasn't the same. Every throw was a little bit here, little bit there, and so that's what you're trying to build. Everyone wants these perfect mechanics, and they say that you get hurt when your mechanics are a little bit off. Okay, so how about you train yourself to be strong enough to when they're off that you're still going to protect yourself?"

After 200 throws, the baseball was tattered, so shredded it was unusable, which meant it was time for McDowell to walk home.

This training approach differed from most White Sox pitchers who, if they stayed in Chicago during the offseason, found a batterymate to work with at Northwestern University and its indoor facilities. The 40-minute drive to Northwestern's campus deterred McDowell. And the self-described loner found something that worked for him.

"I probably was doing it pretty close to every day. Not the entire offseason. But once I started up and started working up to it, yeah, I would go and that's what I did."

McDowell also had a portable mound he pulled from his garage to the alley behind his house. He stayed in shape by pitching off it. In addition to this regimen, McDowell embraced the training methods suggested by the White Sox, relying on biometrics and balance to hone the body. One example: the slide board. Wearing booties, you slide back and forth like a speed skater on a board eight to 12 feet long.

"I still think the slide board's the greatest," McDowell says. "Best baseball exercise that you can get, no matter if you're a pitcher, a player. Everything that you do, you gather your weight on one side, and you explode from one side to the other. If you're pitching, if you're an infielder, if you're hitting—explosion in your first step, it's all about that explosion. Everything [with the slide board] is training off that movement."

Thinking back to his offseason and his conditioning, he grins. "It sounds like such a folklore story."

Insert the sound of a needle scratching across a record.

Before spring training and after months of preparing himself for the season's grind, McDowell sat across from the White Sox front office at an arbitrator's table to decide his compensation for the upcoming season. McDowell disliked the experience, one that minimized his contributions, his buying in to the White Sox' training regimen, and his love for the city—all because the team needed to protect its bottom line.

"It sucks," he says. "It sucks because you have the people that, during the year, you're battling your butt off for, [and] they want you to do well. You want to do well. We're all pulling for the same thing. And then, all of a sudden, it's their job to go in there and *bury* you and try to say, 'You know what? I know he won 17, 20, and 22 games, but you know, that's all stupid, and here's why he sucks, and here's why he shouldn't make this much money."

He pauses.

"It was weird. You were either one of their guys, or you weren't. Kind of like Chicago politics, it seems. Either you're in, or you're not. And I wasn't from day one after the draft. And I don't know why, but it was always contentious."

Indeed, as the fifth overall pick in 1987, McDowell watched as players drafted before and after him signed deals before the White Sox and he discussed a contract.

"They weren't even up to what the guys behind me were getting," McDowell says.

Ten thousand dollars apart on the amount of McDowell's signing bonus, McDowell and the team were at a standoff just before the signing deadline when they negotiated a guaranteed September call-up. This move meant McDowell would earn the major-league minimum salary, a factor in the entire compensation package.

"It's so stupid talking about it now, but *there's* your extra 10,000 to get you up to where everybody else is," he says, shaking his head.

Folklore training, high expectations, and a testy arbitration: the background for Jack McDowell's award-winning season.


## KEYS TO SUCCESS

By 1993, McDowell was a two-pitch pitcher mixing a fastball topping off in the high 80s or low 90s with a forkball 10 miles an hour slower. He threw the fastball 70 percent of the time, and the forkball for the remainder.

Although McDowell was a two-pitch pitcher, Carlton Fisk taught him how to use his fastball in a variety of locations, making him a multifaceted pitcher.

"When I came into the big leagues, Carlton was the one who basically said this guy's got good velocity and good movement on his fastball. We can use it every pitch," McDowell says. "And he taught me how to pitch with my fastball. And as the other stuff developed a couple years into it, that's when, all of a sudden, I jumped to being not just a guy but being one of the better guys."

Lessons learned from Fisk included the importance of pitching with his fastball inside.

"I remember going into my windup and just seeing Carlton shift behind a hitter to where: Where do you go? He wants me to throw it *through* him? Knocking a guy off the plate? Oh. Okay. He was basically teaching me to use my fastball that way. So, you throw it right at the guy's ribs. He'd jump out of the way. And then, the next pitch, you throw a fastball away, and he's done and rolled over. He totally taught me how to use my fastball because he knew that was what I had to offer at that point."

McDowell also used his forkball, a pitch he started throwing in high school and that he developed over time. By changing the wrist angle, he could alter the ball's placement and movement.

"I could stay inside of it like a changeup and make it stay on a plane or make it break a little bit away to a lefty," he says. "If I hooked it, it looked like a slider to a righty. There are a lot of them where you can go look at videos. 'Oh, another slider from McDowell!' No. That's my split."

**Jack McDowell's forkball grip. Courtesy of Jack McDowell.**

He recalls overthrowing one forkball to Kirby Puckett so it cut chest high. Puckett swung and missed. The next day, Puckett jogged past before the game and asked, "What, you're throwing a cutter now?"

With a poker face, McDowell agreed.

"Yeah," he said. "I've been working on it for a while now."

McDowell says his forkball was at its best when, playing catch, he could make the ball flutter like a knuckleball. Knowing how wildly the forkball moves, he recommends pitchers include the pitch in their arsenals.

"Every hitter says it's the toughest pitch in the world to hit because it's unpredictable. Slider? You can have a great slider, but it's still predictable to the point where you know the angle of the break off a guy. Once you've seen him enough, you kind of know what's going on. But a split breaks a little bit different every time. It's just a nasty pitch that varies every time you throw it enough that you can't say, 'Okay, I've seen his split 15 times. Now, I'm going to sit on it.'"

He also sprinkled in a curveball 10 or 12 times a game.

"It was a big, slow curveball that threw everybody off on my other stuff because everything else was the same trajectory."

White Sox pitching coach Jackie Brown helped McDowell refine the curve so he could consistently throw it for a strike.

"It wasn't a putaway," McDowell says. "It was a big breaking ball. So when you see it mixed with my other stuff, it was like, *whoa*! That was cool!"

Brown's tips produced a tighter pitch that triggered early swings.

"They would see [it as] a hanging split," McDowell explains.

In terms of pitch selection, McDowell avoided patterns, so, like his forkball's break, his pitches were unpredictable.

"I would just do things differently. A lot of times, whatever finger went down, I would shake just to do it, just to be different because, at that point, it didn't matter which pitch I threw, I knew I could throw it for a strike, and I knew I could do something. So now, it was like I need to keep everybody on edge. They can't know when I'm going to my split, when I'm just going to go to my fastball. It wasn't like every time I'm 3–1, I'm throwing a split. It just varied. A lot of times, it was pitch to pitch, feel, batter to batter."

He recalls watching video of one game to fine-tune the mechanics of his forkball and recognizing his pattern avoidance.

"I watched for 31 straight fastballs before I saw a split. And, I went, hmm. Maybe that's something I ought to look at. Not be so worried about the split and attack. When you attack, people don't know what to do because no one does that."

Topping it off was an intensity to win that was on constant simmer. Anger fueled McDowell, be it because of the umpire behind the plate ("Oh, I hated them all."), to the front office, to the opposing team. ("I wanted to kick everybody's butt. I didn't want to get a ball signed. I wanted to break their bat with a *ball*.")

One of his catcher's jobs was harnessing that intensity so McDowell executed his pitches. He worked with three catchers in '93, all of whom he praises. He admired Ron Karkovice's arm, defense, and ability to call a game. He liked how Mike LaValliere presented a small target. And,

1993 was Fisk's final season, and McDowell enjoyed his mentor–mentee relationship with the veteran.

"I was never about 'I want my one catcher.' I liked to change it up. I didn't want guys to call the same thing. I was like, mix it up, go wherever you go, and let's see what happens."

With his intensity, McDowell had the reputation as a headhunter. He disagrees with the label.

"I purposely threw at two people in my career. Only two."

Both times were in retaliation for the opposing team hitting McDowell's teammate. The first hitter was Mark Whiten. McDowell threw the ball behind Whiten. Although McDowell missed hitting him, Whiten charged the mound.

"As a pitcher, you kind of think about, "Okay, if this happens, what am I going to do?' And I had all my ideas, but that was ideas based on what happens 99 percent of the time is the guy comes out and tries to tackle you, right?"

Whiten didn't follow the script, though. Once he reached the mound, he stopped in front of McDowell.

"Right at that point, I'm like, 'Yeah, I didn't think about that,'" McDowell says with a laugh.

Whiten swung and landed a punch.

Tit for tat, McDowell punched back.

"It was a hockey fight, and we never went down. And, I'm talking like two and a half, three minutes, and it was jersey to jersey."

Although McDowell wasn't pitching, he observed a hitter–pitcher mound confrontation in 1993, this one featuring teammate Robin Ventura charging 46-year-old Nolan Ryan, and the middle-aged Ryan placing the younger Ventura in a headlock.

Based on the prior game and some chirping between Ventura and the Texas Rangers, McDowell believes Ventura anticipated Ryan plunking him.

"The funny thing is, if you go back and look, you can see exactly what went on in Robin's head," McDowell says. "I've never talked with him about it, but I know this is exactly what happened: If I get hit, I'm going to go out there. The end. I'm going to go out there. Not, if I get hit, I'm going to *kill* him. Not, if I get hit, I'm going to try to break his knee. Not, if I get hit, I'm going to go beat the hell out of him. He didn't go out there with the intention to do bad is what I'm saying. It was kind of more to make a point rather than to go out there because you're so mad you're going to do physical harm. He went out there and just kind of went, 'Oh, crap!' You go look at it, and that's kind of the way it went down."

## 1993

McDowell soared in '93, starting the season with a five-game winning streak and a four-hit shutout against Texas and a two-hit shutout against Oakland. He won 22 games, a remarkable accomplishment under any circumstances but especially in light of the fact that he was pitching with an arthritic hip.

"I had it from the time I was in college," McDowell says. "They told me in college, if you keep pitching, you'll be looking at a hip replacement in your early 30s."

Despite the individual success, McDowell cared more about the team pulling together and winning as a collective.

"Every individual achievement can be improved upon," McDowell says. "And there's only one end-all, and that's winning a championship. That's the only time when you've done everything you can do in that year. Individual achievements, the minute you give up your first hit as a pitcher, you could've had a better year. You could have thrown a no-hitter every single game. The minute you throw your first *ball*. You could have thrown every pitch a strike and thrown a no-hitter every game. You can always get better. The only thing you can't get better at is a championship. Because it's the only time you can stand there and say, 'We can't accomplish nothing more than we did.' And, I guess that's always been my mentality."

Although the White Sox played well, leading the division the entire second half of the season, the 162-game schedule had its bumps. One was the White Sox' release of veteran Carlton Fisk on June 28.

"That's kind of how the White Sox treated people," McDowell says. "Pudge is a lot like me. He was a battler, wasn't their favorite guy. They had contract squabbles, so he was on the outside. The minute he got the games caught thing [passing Bob Boone for most games caught], they released him, and that was that. Meanwhile, we're going to the playoffs,

**Jack McDowell: committed to the team. Courtesy of the National Baseball Hall of Fame and Museum, Cooperstown, N.Y.**

and he's the one that kind of held our hand all the way there, which sucked."

Similar conversations were ongoing with respect to pitcher Bobby Thigpen. In 1990, Thigpen set the record for the most saves in a season with 57, but by 1993, the Chicago papers were publishing stories about trading the onetime premier closer. McDowell says these rumors don't impact the game, but they affect the clubhouse.

"It's definitely a lot more fun when you're in college, and that's your team, and that's going to be your guys, and that's it," McDowell says. "They're not going to *trade* guys. They're not going to release guys. They're your guys, and you're going to fight together."

McDowell embraced the collective approach so far as to bristle when the team made moves at the trading deadline, even though the transactions were meant to address and improve a weakness.

"I'm like, 'That's not the group of guys we came here with!' That was just my mentality, and, consequently, I had a hard time leaving the White Sox. I'm like, 'This is my group of guys I grew up with.'"

As the team closed in on winning the division, the front office considered activating 70-year-old Minnie Miñoso, who played 10 seasons for the Sox in the 1950s and '60s. Doing so would be a public relations move so Miñoso could claim he played in six decades of big-league baseball. McDowell and his teammates questioned the wisdom of the cute window dressing.

"The White Sox hadn't been to the playoffs in a decade, since '83," McDowell says. "We finally had gotten to that point, and they're talking about activating Minnie in September. Just about everybody in the clubhouse didn't get it. He's making a mockery out of what we were doing, and it just didn't seem right. Had we been 15 games out of the race? Okay. Fine. Let's put him in. Get him an at-bat. If you want to get him in this decade, that would make a little more sense."

When players announced they wouldn't play if Miñoso joined the roster, the White Sox front office reconsidered the move.

"I mean, come on," McDowell says. "Randy Johnson was pitching that day. I'm going like, really? So, what if Randy gets pissed that he has to face this guy and drills this 70-year-old? Then what? Then what are we going to see? The whole thing: what a mess."

Another hiccup was when home plate umpire Durwood Merrill ejected McDowell from a game on September 6.

"Durwood usually had the ultra pitchers' zone," McDowell says. "He always had a big zone, and I just thought he missed calls that day. I wanted the zone everyone else got with him. But I wasn't one of his boys."

McDowell recalls an interaction with another home plate umpire, Jim McKean.

"God, I remember in Toronto screaming at him after getting my butt beat by Toronto like I always did," McDowell says, referencing the Blue Jays, the team that beat him twice during the '93 regular season. "After a couple of pitches, I was screaming at him, that he was screwing me, that he was horseshit, that if I'm wrong, throw me out now, half wanting him to throw me out now so I could get the hell out of there. No, I had to go out there and take more pounding. So, he won."

A highlight for the season when McDowell led the league in shutouts (four) was his 20th win when he faced the Minnesota Twins.

"That 20th win was a 10-hit shutout. The nifty 10-hit shutout. They had guys all over the bases every inning. I just happened to get strikeouts at the right time, pitch out of every jam to win my 20th game. To me, that was like, *yeah*! That was the battle. It wasn't this crazy, dominant 17-strikeout game. I never was a huge strikeout guy. Never struck out 200 in a season. It was just hey, if I needed to get outs, I would get outs."

McDowell points out that part of his success was attributable to having a solid defense behind him, including Robin Ventura, who won the Gold Glove at third base in 1993.

"You're going to win and lose games late in games by certain plays that are made," McDowell says. "Basically, a great play is this: You get beat as a pitcher, and someone picks you up on defense. Anytime you get beat and you still get an out, which is why pickoffs are huge. Throwing guys out from behind the plate is huge. Outfield assists are huge."

## OTHER DIMENSIONS

During 1993 and throughout his baseball career, McDowell fought convention. Although a star baseball player, he didn't want to be pigeonholed.

"I never was comfortable being the baseball guy, being the sports guy. Even when you're in college: 'This is Jack. He plays baseball.' Automatic. That's how you're going to get introduced. And I hated that. I didn't want to be that. And I think that's what drove me to the artistic music side to try to submerge myself in that to kind of become more than the baseball guy."

During the season, he took a guitar and a portable four-track recorder with him on road trips.

"I would play a lot and think about music," McDowell says. "Write a lot. Read the local newspaper and see who's in town. Stuff like that. So, yeah, that became my away-from-the-field focus for sure."

He liked visiting cities like Boston, Seattle, and Minneapolis where he could walk around and explore music stores and pick up CDs and sometimes vintage guitars.

"One time, I was in New York, I bought this Gibson acoustic guitar. Incredibly rare. I showed it to Mike Mills of R.E.M., and he's like, 'What the fuck is that? That's sick!'"

McDowell played in a couple of rock bands, first V.I.E.W. and later Stickfigure with Mike Mesaros, formerly of the Smithereens, and Michael Hamilton. He toured with Stickfigure in '93, and he says music was a great release for him. And baseball opened some music doors for McDowell. *Ray Gun* magazine contacted him and asked if he would be willing to interview someone for them. His response? Yes, if the subject is Paul Westerberg of the Replacements.

"That was really cool."

McDowell laughs, though. "It's the same thing when I'm hanging with any rock guys that are sports guys. They want to talk about sports. I want to talk about music."

Part of '93 included McDowell in music headlines for his involvement in a late-night New Orleans scuffle. After attending an Urge Overkill concert with Pearl Jam lead singer Eddie Vedder, the two moved to another club and another show by the Specials before winding down the night. Then, a Pearl Jam "fan" confronted Vedder about the band selling out.

"Eddie was at that point where they had gotten to where he had become a little bit famous. Still believed in the goodness of everybody and believed he could convince everybody that hey, we're doing the right thing. We're not sellouts. So, he took on this guy in talking to him," McDowell says.

Vedder's confronter didn't accept the explanation, and, later in the night, he approached Vedder again.

"As we're getting ready to leave, the guy follows [Vedder] outside and starts really getting into it, like he wants to get after him. So, they start getting kind of chest to chest, and all of a sudden, they go. And so, I jumped in and went also. Then the bouncer of the club we were in decided to come up behind me and smoke me from behind. Cheap-shotted me, and [I] ended up hitting my head on a *car* bumper and getting knocked out."

McDowell thought justice was served, though, when the bouncer, suing Vedder, showed up for a court hearing and was arrested on an outstanding warrant.

## SETTING THE TONE

Looking back on the '93 team, McDowell describes it as his and Robin Ventura's. The former college baseball rivals from Stanford and Oklahoma State, respectively, set the tone.

"We kind of grew up together," McDowell says.

When the White Sox drafted Ventura, McDowell immediately contacted his new teammate and offered to show him the ropes.

"I just knew from my experience; I knew nothing, nobody, and didn't know what to do."

So that Ventura would avoid the same predicament, he was invited to live in McDowell's house for spring training. From there, they built a friendship and a commitment to win.

"We were the guys, and I think that was part of the deal," McDowell says. "People would say that a pitcher can't be a leader and this or that, and I absolutely was on that team. I always saw myself more as a position player and an everyday guy, and I was at it every day. Where, a lot of pitchers, they pitch their game and they're all fired up and then they're screwing around for four days, playing jokes and all this. I was on the top step, screaming at the other pitcher every inside pitch. I wanted to win every game. I wanted to win. And so, I think that had a lot to do with our attitude and our drive and everyone else feeling they needed to step up to that."

McDowell instilled this spirit not by calling team meetings or confronting teammates whose drive wasn't as stoked as his.

"It was just the way we went about it," he says. "The way I went about it, my will to win, my will to compete. My will to fight. My will not to take any crap from anybody, and it was all about every day, we were going to win a ballgame, and it didn't matter how we got there. If we had to kill somebody at second base, if we had to run over a catcher, if we had to drill somebody. Whatever we had to do to win, I'm going to be pushing for that. So, it was more that, when I went out there, this guy doesn't have the best stuff. But did everybody play better because he was there? Yeah. Because they were kind of scared not to because of what I brought to the table."

McDowell clarifies that teammates didn't play harder behind him when he pitched. Instead, he describes it as raising their play to another level, feeding off his intensity.

"They knew I was leaving it on the field at all costs," he says. "They knew that I was the guy that was going to protect them if I needed to, and they knew on the other four days, I probably wanted to win more than when I pitched. That pays off. It really does. I tried to instill that in the pitchers I've dealt with. You've got your team behind you, you won't understand how much better it is."

In terms of cultivating this kind of passion, McDowell questions whether you can. It's how he's hardwired.

"I think a lot of it has to do with makeup. I really do. I think you can tame a stallion a lot more than making a sheep a stallion. I think it's tough to take guys out of their comfort level."

He pauses.

"You can kind of calm the guys that are over the top, but I don't think you win with the sheep. You win with the guys you need to calm down a little bit."

Not only did McDowell drive the team with his intensity, but he was also attentive to the details of pitching and ways he could obtain an advantage. For example, he focused on his pickoff move.

"I always had good feet, and I always had a good move, but I worked on it," he says. "I knew I wasn't a slide-step guy, so I was going to be a 1–4 or a 1–5. So, I learned how to keep the running game in check by varying it. Vary the looks. How does it look to the runner when you go home? Now, you've got to come up with pickoff moves off of that. It's a simple idea, but no one pays attention to it."

In addition to McDowell and Ventura setting the tone, manager Gene Lamont earned American League Manager of the Year honors for how he oversaw his team.

"He let us play. He recognized what we had, what our strengths were, and basically did the right things all the time. There were situations that popped up, obviously. No one heard about them. We handled them in house. He did a great job of that."

Asked about what stands out about the season when he was named the American League's best pitcher, McDowell answers, his team finally reaching the playoffs.

"Getting over the hump of being in the West with the killer A's teams of the '90s," he says. "Those are the days before the wild card, and you had to win the division outright, and we had to beat a team that was throwing a bunch of Hall of Famers and a bunch of All-Stars out there every day. And we're a young team coming up and trying to get over the hump, and that was the year we finally did it."

After winning the division, the team faced the Toronto Blue Jays in the American League Championship Series. With McDowell struggling against the Jays during the regular season, there was discussion about tweaking the rotation and emphasizing Wilson Alvarez, who beat them twice in 1993. But Lamont ultimately went with the rotation he used and that won during the regular season, starting McDowell in Game One. McDowell pitched into the seventh inning at Comiskey Park, giving up 13 hits and seven runs. The result? Blue Jays 7, White Sox 3.

"I'm not saying that was right or wrong," McDowell says. "And I'm sure if they didn't go with me, I would've been pissed and put up a big stink, and I'm wondering how much that had to do with it. But I got beat twice. They just got me real good."

He shakes his head.

"It's a freakin' All-Star team!" he says of the ultimate World Series winners. "They didn't suck when you're going [John] Olerud, [Roberto] Alomar, [Tony] Fernandez, Kelly Gruber, Joe Carter, Devon White. Rickey Henderson—is that good?" He laughs.

Nonetheless, McDowell was a workhorse in 1993, throwing 256 2/3 innings and pitching 10 complete games, second and third most in the league, respectively. For this longevity, he credits his offseason practice of multiple throws from various positions as building *all* muscles in his arm and shoulder, and, when he thinks about today's practice of limiting pitch counts, he bristles and encourages people to absorb lessons from history.

"Every big-name pitcher in the '70s and '80s just stayed healthy their whole career. Think about it. All the top guys threw a ton of innings and stayed healthy. Nowadays, you can't do that. These guys claim they have the answers. Well, this pitch count and this limit and this innings limit—how's that working for us? Ever since this limiting throwing has come into the game, do we have more injuries now, or do we have fewer injuries now? More times 10. This ain't working."

## NEXT STEPS

Just as the '93 season began with arbitration, so did its end. With arbitration hearings as bookends, McDowell is puzzled by the White Sox's handling of his employment terms.

"In situations where everybody else in the game was getting multiyear deals and being pumped up as the faces of the organization, I'm getting taken to arbitration and told I'm a piece of crap."

Consecutive one-year deals and arbitration proceedings began to take a toll on McDowell.

"Look at my front part of 1994," McDowell says. "I came back after doing what I did for those three, four years and said, 'Okay. I'm going to show them. I'm going to do more.' Well, what the hell else more was I going to do? And so, I came out there and scuffled the front end of '94."

By the end of May, McDowell's record was two wins, seven losses, and a 6.24 earned-run average.

"I remember sitting in the outfield one day [during 1994] and going, 'You know what, guys? I just did the math, and, if I break the Hershiser record of consecutive scoreless innings, I will just break 4 [for an ERA].' And, everybody's cracking up. That's pretty daunting to go into the rest of the season knowing that."

McDowell ended the season strong, though. His ERA for the year? 3.73.

"I didn't do it all straight," he says, referencing Hershiser's run.

One way he turned things around was by consulting sports psychologist Jim Fannin. Teammate Kirk McCaskill worked with Fannin previously and suggested McDowell talk with him. McDowell agreed.

"The funny thing was everything I learned from him and everything he had to say, I was going, 'That was my thought process. That was always my thought process.' That was what I lost."

Fannin worked with McDowell to sharpen his focus.

"He had to bring me back to stop being a pussy and go back to doing what you used to do. Which was to focus to do this, to attack to do that, and I'm going, 'Yeah, this is exactly how I used to do it.' Some people need to be taught that. I had the killer thing and that competitive thing out of my gourd, you know?"

Although McDowell turned his season around, 1994 ended abruptly because of the players' strike resulting in no World Series being played. And, as an assistant player representative, McDowell learned that, based on revenues, his salary should have been doubled.

"The most amazing thing about being a player rep is being in the meeting where we had just broken the $3 million barrier, and then, all of a sudden, it went up to like *five*, and they were like, 'Yeah, right now, you should be a $10 million player.' And, they showed us charts of revenues and players' salaries, and everybody in the room was almost rolling. Just going, 'Are you effing kidding me that there's supposed to be a $10 million player?'"

After McDowell won 91 games for the White Sox over seven seasons, the team traded him to the New York Yankees for the 1995 season. McDowell describes his new team as gamers. "Really good guys top to bottom. Not the craziest talented group, but solid enough to get the first wild card."

When Yankee pitcher Jimmy Key suffered an injury during his fifth start and was lost for the rest of the season, manager Buck Showalter approached McDowell.

"I'm going to need you to be an innings eater," Showalter said. "I know you're a team guy and don't care about your stats. We're going to have to ride you."

"That's fine," McDowell said, understanding that the Yankees were thin on pitching. He performed the role asked of him. He stayed in some games where he gave up five or six runs, but, if the pitching staff had had more depth, he would've been pulled sooner. Despite his shouldering the burden, Yankees fans were unsympathetic.

"I had a couple of bad starts in a row, and then here comes the White Sox. The team that traded me. Beating the hell out of me. And my team booing me at the same time. Because I stayed in there for three home runs and like seven runs in six innings. Meanwhile, everybody else in baseball is out after three innings and saving their stats and coming back fresh the next start. So yeah, I snapped. Snapped a gasket."

As Showalter replaced McDowell with another pitcher and McDowell walked toward the dugout, the boos poured down. And McDowell raised his hand and extended his middle finger to the crowd.

Even though headlines blared about "Jack the Flipper" and magazines dissected his gesture, McDowell marched on and pitched strongly. He finished the regular season with 15 wins, 10 losses, and a 3.93 ERA. And he pitched in the deciding game of the American League Division Series against the Seattle Mariners, entering the game in relief of David Cone in the bottom of the ninth inning. The game was tied at 4, with one out and baserunners at second and first base.

McDowell first faced Edgar Martinez. After five pitches: strikeout.

The next hitter was Alex Rodriguez, who hit into a fielder's choice. Out of the jam, out of the inning.

"I pitched with a tear in my lat muscle," McDowell says. "It was about the size of a golf ball. That's the way it goes. But that's what we did back then. And Coney was scuffling his butt off, too. He was sore as hell and torn up as well."

McDowell pauses.

"Randy Johnson was doing the same thing. He was throwing a ton of innings. He came in in relief and threw a bunch of innings on one day rest. It was just the way it was. You competed. You went out there. It wasn't about your career. It wasn't about your longevity. It was about right *there*! We're *here*! We're in the playoffs. We might as well take a chance."

After the Yankees lost in the bottom of the 11th, with Martinez hitting a double to drive in Joey Cora, McDowell returned to the locker room and cried.

"I kept looking at [Don] Mattingly," McDowell says. "I knew he was retiring, and I knew this was his only shot [at playing in a World Series], and it tore me up."

Cone was similarly upset. The two pitchers then commiserated.

"You know," Cone said. "If we had won that game, what the hell were we going to do when we went to Cleveland? Who was going to pitch?"

McDowell looked at him and laughed.

"No shit," he said. "It would have been, okay—now what?"

McDowell spent only one season in New York before signing as a free agent with the Cleveland Indians, a team stacked with superstars like Albert Belle, Jim Thome, and Manny Ramirez but, unlike the White Sox and Yankees, lacking team spirit.

"We had too many guys going different directions," McDowell says. "I asked John Hart, I said get me out of here. Trade me. It was horrible. I said this is the worst thing I've ever been a part of. I hated every minute of it. The only thing that kept me sane was being friends with Charlie Nagy and getting along with a couple of guys, but what a mess."

In Cleveland, McDowell began feeling some discomfort in his elbow. He went in for a surgery to relieve pressure on a nerve near the elbow, but during the surgery, his nerve was severed. After that, he pitched at less than 100 percent.

"It was like pitching without a ligament. And you can go on for so long, and then it's not going to happen. I pieced together two years of not making a whole lot of starts. By doing that, tore my shoulder up. At that point, I was like, ah, that's enough."

As a result, McDowell retired from baseball at age 33.

"I was more of a loner, and I just kind of took off and disappeared and did my own thing. I didn't stay in touch with a ton of people. I look at it now and go, 'Oh, that's kind of stupid.' But it's a weird lifestyle. Guys are from different places. And, the same old joke, at the end of the season, you-get-to-pick-your-own-friends-type deal."

After spending 12 seasons in the major leagues and then coaching young players, McDowell has several strong opinions about the game, one of which is the de-emphasis of the split-finger fastball or forkball that he used with success. As an example, he points out that, as a minor-league manager, he was advised *not* to teach young pitchers the split.

"They were like nah, nah, nah. If he makes it to Double A, we can teach it to him then. I'm like going—this guy's repertoire—he's a sinker-slider guy. If he could throw a split right now, you're talking about a big-league closer."

McDowell says the fear of the pitch triggering injuries is unfounded.

"The most durable guys of the '80s were fastball-split guys. Jack Morris, me, [Rick] Aguilera. I mean, come on. It hurts? According to who? Nobody's done a study on that that says why. It's so many people putting their stamp on something."

Another topic McDowell has an opinion about is performance-enhancing drugs. His approach is, put yourself in a player's shoes and being told that, if you take this substance, you'll return from an injury and be back on the field quicker and stronger. Who would reject that treatment?

"It wasn't put in front of me," McDowell says. "It wasn't *out* with any of the teams I played with like some of the other teams it was. Obviously helped a ton of guys. The way I look at it: 80 percent of the guys were on it, so what are you going to do? I'm talking Hall of Fame stuff and all of that. Come on. They hold [Roger] Clemens and [Barry] Bonds up like they're the only two guys who did it. I'm like, you're putting in guys every year . . . what are you doing?"

He also questions the game's new emphasis on statistics.

"With all of the knowledge and all the stats and all the things they're doing now compared to what we did back then, are you getting people out at a better rate? Is the guy leading the league in hitting hitting .210? It's all the same. You've got to execute right there. With all the information, it's a competition between two guys, and you just go at it. Information? Blah. Overrated."

One thing statistics can't measure is team spirit and good chemistry.

"They can't put a number to any of that stuff," McDowell says. "And so they want to make it like that doesn't matter so they can stay in business. But guess what? You ain't winning without that. We could've won two more games if we had put the right lineup there every day. Well, you can win 12 more if you're all pulling together for 162, you dumbasses."

Looking back, he questions whether he would do things differently as a player. Like his hatred of umpires.

"I wonder how things would have been if I hadn't been such a red ass and all and hating everybody," he says. "I know that's definitely not what I would teach. It's not a healthy way to go about it. It's just what I was."

McDowell now lives in Charlotte, North Carolina, with his wife Carrie and his three youngest children, Molly, Rhett, and Rory. He has fun by taking in a Panthers football game with his family, and he enjoys sharing what he knows about baseball. Coaching, he discovered, produces results when you are sincere, passionate, and respectful.

"There's different ways to get to different people. Unless you know how to do it, you can be a hard-ass, wow, great. He's a hard-ass. What a great leader. No, that's a bunch of crap. You need to know how to get guys comfortable to be their best."

When he returned to coaching a few years ago, McDowell sought the advice of his former manager Jeff Torborg.

"Be yourself," Torborg said. "Let it fly. You've got everything to offer. Just be yourself."

Charting his own path—something McDowell has always done and done well.

# 8

# FINDING 75: BARRY ZITO

## 2002 AMERICAN LEAGUE CY YOUNG AWARD

*When I interviewed Barry Zito in April 2016, he was in his first year away from playing baseball and in his first full-time year of pursuing a new career in music. He said that now that he was away from baseball, he had more room available on his hard-drive space for requests like mine, to look back when he was the best at his craft and to explore what made him successful and what stands out to him from this time. So we drank black coffee and munched on crisp green apples at the Well Coffeehouse outside of Nashville and talked about baseball and challenges and growth and how perspectives evolve. Zito had some time to reflect before he had to leave—he was meeting with some other songwriters that morning to craft some music.*

One month into the 2002 season, Barry Zito was slumping. With one win and one loss, he took the mound at Yankee Stadium on April 30.[1] His challenges continued as, in the bottom of the first inning, he gave up six runs. Lasting four innings that night, his line score was six runs, six hits, four walks, and six strikeouts in 96 pitches. Dejected, he returned to his hotel room, now 1–2 with a 4.81 earned-run average.

Zito looked at himself in the mirror. He replayed the first inning in his head. With the score tied at 0 and runners on first and second and two outs, Jorge Posada tapped the ball back to Zito, a grounder he normally would field and throw to first to get out of the inning, but the ball skipped between his legs.

"Then all these runs came in," he says. "I was completely demoralized."[2]

Zito moved his face closer to the glass, his brown eyes looking within, and he said, "Be a man."

He thought about his season so far and the six games he had pitched. Game One was against Texas at home followed by another a game against the Rangers on the road. For his third start, he faced the Angels on the road, and then he pitched against them at Oakland. Games five and six were against the Yankees.

"It sucks as a starting pitcher to face the same teams twice in a row. And then, to do that three straight times?" Zito says. "I think mentally I was already a little bit beat. I would get in my own head about things like that."

Still staring at himself, tired of the way his season was progressing and committed to turning things around, Zito repeated, "Be a fucking man."

In hindsight, he says, "That sounds so . . . whatever. 'Be a man.' But I felt like I was being a little bitch out there. Sometimes, you go out there, and you're a pussy. And you get in your own way. You're afraid to take risks. You're worried about things you can't control. You're worried about the future. Everything's getting in the way of your talent."

Determined to treat each start like a bar fight, Zito next faced the White Sox in New Comiskey Park. He pitched six innings and earned the win.

"I gave up an opposite field home run to Frank Thomas on a really good pitch down and away," Zito says. "But I was like, okay." Step one in the right direction was complete, and his record was even at 2–2.

Beating Chicago was the first of nine straight wins for Zito. Going into the All-Star break, his record was 11 wins and three losses. He had lowered his ERA to 3.49. And he was on his way to winning the American League Cy Young Award, something that seemed plausible before the rough April beginning.

"I was coming off a really hot run in '01 that I had had the year before," he says. "The last two months of the season in '01, I was the AL Pitcher of the Month. And then I pitched a game in the playoffs. Lost 1–0. So I was coming off a pretty crazy run."

Within this context, Zito sat down with fellow starters Tim Hudson and Mark Mulder for a preseason interview with *San Francisco Chroni-*

*cle* beat writer Susan Slusser. The group discussed how Hudson finished second in the Cy Young Award voting in 2000. Mulder did the same in 2001.

"Oh," someone said. "I guess it's Zito's turn to get second place."

Zito thought to himself, "Well, let's just wait on that one."

He had experienced success and knew he was capable of more. He needed to execute, and that's what he focused on, his focus especially acute after his rough April start.


## DRAWN TO THE MOUND

Zito discovered baseball when he was six years old. His family moved from Las Vegas to San Diego so his mother could serve as pastor at a church. New in town, his father Joe took Barry to a T-ball field, and Barry, knowing nothing about baseball, ran to the pitcher's mound.

Seeing his son had an affinity to throw accurately, Joe, a former manager of entertainment acts, pushed Barry. He made his son practice every day. Occasionally, Barry protested and said he wanted to play with his friends rather than practice.

"Do you want to be in the major leagues?" Joe asked. "Do you want to be a champion?"

"Yes," Barry answered.

"Well, this is what champions do. Champions don't stop working to go play with their friends. They get their work done."

Zito appreciates his dad's dedication and how he applied lessons learned from management to his son's interest in baseball.

"He always said, 'Until you're 18, we're going to do this. Once you're 18 and you want to quit baseball and never play again, that's fine. But we've gotta make it there and give yourself the best chance.'"

Zito pauses.

"My dad's thing was, until 12-year-olds run the world, he's going to tell you what to do."

The elder Zito arranged for his son to receive pitching lessons from 1976 National League Cy Young Award winner Randy Jones. Zito worked with Jones beginning when he was 12 until he was 17.

"My parents couldn't afford anything," Zito says. "I mean, my mom was a minister. My father was not working. And they really didn't have anything saved, so I remember they would be scraping up the 50 dollars a week that it was and drive about 45 minutes up to Poway, which is where Randy lived."

He shakes his head.

"My parents always figured out a way to get the money for that. I was always impressed by that. They made it a huge priority in my life. They sacrificed a lot."

Zito liked Jones as a teacher. He could joke and make the teenager relax, but he also had the ability to get his attention.

"Come on, lefty!" Jones would bark, then spit tobacco juice at Zito's shoes. "Do it right!"

Jones emphasized proper mechanics and repetition to ensure that the lessons stuck. He told Zito to practice his motion in front of a full-length mirror by throwing balled-up socks at the glass.

"Throw it," Jones said. "Throw it, throw it, throw it. Get all those reps in."

By the time he was a high school senior, Zito had a great curveball he taught himself from reading Tom Seaver's book *The Art of Pitching*. Although he topped out at only 82 miles per hour, he attracted the interest of Seattle Mariners scout Craig Weissman. Weissman approached Zito and asked if he was interested in being drafted in the eighth round and signing with the Mariners.

"No," Zito said. "I want to be drafted in the first round."

Weissman looked at the high schooler and replied, "Everyone does."

Despite being rebuffed, Weissman saw promise in Zito, and Weissman tutored him. To increase speed, Weissman reworked Zito's delivery, shifting him from an over-the-top approach to a three-quarters arm angle. He also made the delivery more compact by reducing Zito's leg kick.

The results were immediate.

"In two months, my velocity went up to 87," Zito says. "Then, that fall at UC–Santa Barbara, I hit 90, and then the following January, the first series of the year, I was pitching out of the bullpen. And I hit 93. I gained 10 miles an hour in about eight months. At that point, I was like, wow. I could actually have a chance at pitching in the big leagues."

Two years later, the Oakland A's selected Zito in the first round, the ninth overall pick. Excited to be in professional baseball, Zito knew little about the A's organization.

"I grew up a Padres fan. The A's were in the other league. I always thought the unis were cool."

The A's invited their first-round pick to Oakland–Alameda County Coliseum to work out with the major-league team and throw a bullpen session. Zito put on a uniform, and he trotted to the outfield grass and began his stretching routine. Holding three baseballs in each hand, he extended his arms parallel to the ground. He began a series of small, tight circles, gradually increasing the circumference.

"I swear that's why I never had arm problems," Zito says. "I mean, who knows, but I always had a ton of blood pumping in my body before I even threw a ball."

His exercise caught the attention of A's relief pitcher Billy Taylor.

"Hey!" Taylor screamed. "What the fuck are you doing, man?"

Zito assumed Taylor's comments were directed at him, but he pressed on with his stretches.

"I'm like, 'Oh, God,'" Zito remembers. "'I'm not stopping. That's my routine, and I've got to throw a bullpen.'"

"What is that shit?" Taylor hollered.

Zito pressed on, committed to the routine that brought him this far.

Welcome to professional baseball, kid.


## CHARGING THROUGH THE MINORS

Drafted in '99, Zito progressed rapidly, spending six weeks in high-A ball, then moving to Double A, then reaching Triple A all in his first professional season.

"All the Triple-A guys went to the big leagues in September," he says. "Their team was in the playoffs, so they had a short roster. So, we flew into Colorado Springs [from Double A], bright eyed and bushy tailed. I started that game. It was the last day of the Triple-A season. Went six innings, gave up a run, won the game. And then pitched through the playoffs and won the Triple-A World Series that year. So that was like, surreal."

Zito became a more complete pitcher in the minor leagues thanks in part to A's pitching coordinator Ron Romanick, who showed Zito the four-seam changeup.

"I had always thrown a two-seam changeup. But it just faded, like a screwball too much. A lot of people think your changeup needs to be about movement. I mean, your changeup doesn't even move one inch off a straight-line trajectory if you have the right arm speed and release. It's probably going to be more effective if it doesn't move because the hitter won't pick it up. But he helped me to try to keep that four-seam rotation of my changeup so the hitters can't pick up the wobble of the seams."

While he progressed in the minors, Zito had fun. He was happy to be playing baseball professionally, and he didn't dwell on when he might be called up to the big leagues. But his time in the minors was brief. In 2000, only his second year of pro ball, the A's called Zito up for good. Although they needed a pitcher to face the Colorado Rockies in Denver, a notoriously unfavorable setting for pitchers, the A's opted to call up Marcus Jones for that start rather than Zito.

"I found out later they didn't want to bring up one of their prospects and get a shellacking in Colorado, which is the worst experience in baseball," Zito says.

Instead, for his big-league debut, Zito faced the Anaheim Angels, an incredibly stacked lineup with Troy Glaus, Tim Salmon, and Mo Vaughn. The night before his start, Zito flew into Oakland and, from the airport Hilton bar's TV, watched Tim Hudson face the Angels.

"Huddy was getting hit around that night," Zito says. "I'm watching Tim Hudson, a guy who had come up the year before, and he was just taking the league by storm. So I was like, wow. That sucks. I'm getting a little nervous."

The next day, Zito stepped on the mound on a sunny July day and fired his first pitch to catcher Ramon Hernandez.

The public address announcer said, "First pitch, one oh seven."

As Hernandez threw the ball back to Zito, Zito thought, "Are they joking because I'm the new guy, and I'm trying to throw 107? That was weird—they really made a joke out of that."

Later, he realized the PA announcer was referencing the *time* when the first pitch was thrown, not its speed.

Zito pitched five innings that day. In his final inning, he walked the first batter, gave up a single, and then walked the next hitter. With the bases loaded and no outs, pitching coach Rick Peterson visited Zito on the mound. Peterson whispered, "Hey, Z."

Zito leaned closer to hear the message.

"Man, just act like it's a wave you're riding," Peterson said in a low voice. "You're down at the beach riding those waves."

He patted Zito and returned to the dugout.

Zito took a deep breath. He watched for the signs from Hernandez as he faced Mo Vaughn, the 1995 American League Most Valuable Player.

He struck Vaughn out. One out.

Next up was Tim Salmon, the power-hitting right fielder who clubbed 34 home runs in 2000.

Salmon struck out.

Next up: Garrett Anderson, a three-time All-Star and two-time Silver Slugger. Four pitches later, Zito struck out Anderson. Inning over, no runs, and out of the jam.

Although Zito was finished for the day, manager Art Howe sent him to the mound to warm up for the sixth inning. Before Zito threw a pitch, Howe stepped out of the dugout and signaled for the bullpen.

"He did that just to pull me off to get an ovation. Because Art Howe was just a gentleman. That was just magical."

## FINDING 75

Since high school, Zito had worn 34 as his jersey number. He picked 34 because of right-handed pitcher Kris Benson, the number one overall pick in the 1996 draft.

"His delivery was the most perfect mechanical delivery I had ever seen, so I started wearing 34 because of Kris."

When Zito joined the A's, 34 wasn't available—the A's retired it to honor Hall of Fame alumnus Rollie Fingers. Being a rookie and having no say in his uniform number, Zito accepted 53 with a smile.

The following season, though, equipment manager Steve Vucinich asked Zito which number he wanted.

"I just started going through the numbers in my head of what looks best with Zito on top of it. The aesthetics or symmetrics. So, it was 57 or 75 because I thought they looked best with that little shelf on top, but 57 was going to give me a lower chance of keeping it for my career, so I picked 75."

As he settled into the big leagues, Zito clicked with fellow starter Tim Hudson. Hudson was the first of the A's Big Three starters (Mark Mulder, Hudson, and Zito) to reach the big leagues, and he achieved immediate success, winning 20 games in 2000.

"If Huddy wasn't pitching, we would be screwing around and laughing, talking about something that was completely irrelevant to the game," Zito says.

One time, the young pitchers were in the dugout, cutting up while the A's were losing. As closer Jason Isringhausen passed them on the way to the bullpen, he stared at them. Without saying one word, Isringhausen quieted the pitchers with his intense glare. That and his physical strength his young teammates were well aware of.

"We stopped fooling around," Zito says. "We used to call Izzy 'Dum Dum' because he had superhuman strength. You do not want him mad at you."

In addition to teaching lessons about how to conduct oneself, Isringhausen looked after Zito.

"When you're 22 years old and having some success in the big leagues, there's not really a governor on anything. You feel like you can do anything," Zito says.

Like a big brother, Isringhausen reminded Zito to be smart. Don't stay out too late. Don't put yourself in a bad situation. Take a cab home if you've been drinking.

If Isringhausen played a brotherly role, then Scott Hatteberg was the father.

"He had a huge influence on me," Zito says. "[Adam] Piatt and I used to call him Daddyberg because he was like a dad. Me and Adam were running around and going crazy, and Scott's a collared shirt, starch, perfectly cuffed sleeves, and a little chest hair and perfectly coiffed. Man, we used to give him shit. We were like, 'Dude, you are such a dad. Look at your outfit now.'"

Hatteberg turned to his young teammates and grimaced. "Would you two shut up?"

In spite of the ribbing, Hatteberg guided his young teammates toward refined big-league tastes. When he saw Zito pouring sweetener into his coffee, Hatteberg stopped him.

"No, no, no," Hatteberg said.

"What?" Zito asked.

"You're ruining the bean!" Hatteberg said. "You're ruining the essence of the coffee bean! You're going to put that shit in there?"

Zito looked at him and shrugged.

"Do you realize how hard someone had to work to get this fine coffee? No. Quit putting that stuff in there."

Zito laughs. "I drink my coffee black to this day because Scott used to yell at me."

David Justice, in his 14th and final major-league season, also stood out as a role model, a seasoned veteran who carried himself with class.

"Dave was the most groomed, always smelled good, and there wasn't a hair out of place, and fingernails manicured. Spoke so eloquently, perfect teeth. Dave was just like from another planet."

The pro Justice laughed at Zito and Piatt cutting up.

"You guys remind me of Ron Gant and me when we were first coming up with the Braves," Justice said. Which led Justice to share stories about being on the successful Atlanta teams during the 1990s, a treat for Zito. After all, he grew up watching Braves games on TV—the only games available at the time. Now he was spending time with a player he admired as a teen.

The architect behind this roster was general manager Billy Beane.

"I like Billy," Zito says. "He's always somebody I enjoy talking to."

Zito remembers Beane spending time in the weight room on the treadmill. A former player, Beane had no problem flipping shit to the players he added to the roster.

"Barry," Beane said one time. "You were terrible last night. Just serving them up to Manny."

Zito stood there, stunned, uncertain what to say after hearing this message from the big boss.

"Come on, man," Beane said. "We're fine. Relax."

Zito likes how personable Beane is and also how bold and assertive he is.

"The guy has balls," Zito says. "He's going to do what he wants to do. Because he believes in it. That's something I have a lot of respect for."

## FOCUS

After a rookie season in 2000 when he won seven games, threw his first shutout, and posted a 2.72 ERA, Zito was off to a great start. But by mid-2001, he wasn't pleased with his results. His record was around .500, and his earned-run average was plump. After the Minnesota Twins lit him up in consecutive games, Zito thought the A's would send him back to Triple A for more seasoning.

"I was terrified to take the mound," Zito says.

Zito's dad met with his son to get him back on track. In between starts, they read and discussed a book, *The Creative Mind*, by Ernest Holmes, written in 1919.

"In a nutshell, it's like God or the universal force or whatever you want to call it, can be used in a certain way, can be accessed to give you what you need," Zito says. "Now, as a Christian, years later, it sounds like a very selfish thing, but at the time, I had crazy results with it."

After the two read the book, Joe asked, "Do you see yourself as the best pitcher in the league?"

Barry shook his head no. "How can I? I freaking suck. I just got lit up."

"Well," Joe said. "You've got to change the inside before you're going to see any of the outside change."

Barry listened.

"You've got to see yourself differently. You've got to carry yourself differently. You've got to relate to your teammates differently. Like, 'Yeah! Not only do I deserve to be here, I'm the frickin' best guy on the team!' Not in an arrogant way, but in an assured way."

Zito agreed to apply the principles. The next day, he met Rick Peterson for a bullpen, and the pitching coach shared a mechanical tweak to fine-tune Zito's control. The adjustment clicked. Coupling it with Zito's new focus, Zito ended the last two months of the season with 11 wins and one loss.

"It's like crazy domination," Zito says.

Zito then resumed his usual offseason routine.

"I'd start throwing in November. Throw bullpens in December. Then, I'd go to Alan Jaeger's camp in January. I've worked with Alan since '98."

At Jaeger's camp, Zito spent his mornings doing yoga, an exercise he encourages all pitchers to implement into their regimen.

"Having more flexibility is always going to help," Zito says. "I think the guys that are the hardest throwers have the most mobility through the spine. They can rotate and wind up, and I always had terrible rotation through my spine. So, I needed [yoga] to try and just stay even par on people."

After lunch, he stretched more, doing arm circles, tubing, and playing catch that progressed to long toss, throwing the ball 320–330 feet. He acknowledges two schools of thought regarding long toss. Opponents point to long toss altering a pitcher's release point and thus possibly skewing his mechanics. Zito, though, liked the freedom he felt when his body worked to throw a ball nearly half a city block to hit his target.

Prior to 2002, Zito also worked with Dr. Michael Clark, who emphasized strengthening isolated muscle groups, working on a single leg, one arm, the hips. Then he headed for spring training where he resumed learning lessons from A's pitching coach Rick Peterson.

"I really like Rick Peterson," Zito says. "He's kind of different, and one thing that I really admire about him, especially as I've gotten older, is he does what he does, and he's kind of take it or leave it."

Peterson tailored his approach and instructions based on a particular pitcher's needs.

"He took who you were and made a couple of tweaks. He wasn't trying to force guys into becoming his mold or something."

Zito points to the pitchers who resurrected their careers after working with Peterson as evidence of his strengths.

"Jason Isringhausen. He was kind of a loose cannon with the Mets. Never had a ton of success. Came over to Oakland. Got with Rick. Saved 40 games—I mean, stud. The next year: Billy Koch, 2002. He had some good years in Toronto. Had his best year with the A's. Next year, Keith Foulke in 2003 had his best year with the A's. Those are not coincidences."

One way Peterson helped Zito was by shifting where he stood on the mound.

"He moved me over from the first-base side of the mound to the third-base side, and that changed everything for me. Because I was a fastball-in guy to righties. So, when I was on the third-base side, I could get in to righties much easier. And then it gave my curveball a chance to stay on the plate instead of when I was way over on the first-base side, it would sweep across. It wouldn't really have a lot of time in the zone. So that was a huge adjustment Rick made for me."

Zito also likes how Peterson held scouting meetings for the pitching staff as they began a series against a new team. It facilitated pitchers and catchers getting on the same page about hitters' strengths and weaknesses, and it helped the battery stay in sync for pitch selections during the game.

## 2002

In 2002, Zito threw three pitches: fastball, curveball, and changeup. To right-handed hitters, he threw inside 60 percent of the time and away the remainder. To lefties, he threw away 80 percent.

"I had kind of a mental block about [throwing inside to left-handers]. I would go down and away mostly to lefties. Some guys, man, like A. J. Pierzynski and Doug Mientkiewicz, were two lefties that played for the Twins. Man, I would throw to those guys, and all day long I would hit them. I'd try to aim it in there, but I must have hit Mientkiewicz five times that season. Yeah. I didn't like throwing in to lefties."

Although Zito's curveball with its huge break received most of the spotlight and hype in 2002, he points to his changeup as a key factor in his success.

"I felt I could throw my changeup for strikes probably seven out of 10 times. And I think that's why I won the Cy Young. Everyone focuses on my curveball, but the changeup set up the fastball. I mean, if someone has a good changeup and a fastball, they can dominate. If you add a plus breaking pitch in there too, at that point, it's unfair."

Catcher Ramon Hernandez worked with Zito for roughly two-thirds of his starts. The two were in sync.

"Ramon knew me inside out. I'll still look at game tapes from that '01–'02 run, and I'm not shaking almost ever. I mean, Ramon was putting down what I had thought in my head seconds before. It was crazy how locked in we were."

They worked together so much that Hernandez learned Zito liked throwing curveballs in 2–2 counts and, when it was 3–2, to signal for either a fastball or a changeup.

Zito also enjoyed pitching to backup Greg Myers.

"Greg was the salty vet," Zito says. "Crash Davis we used to call him. He was this good-looking, chiseled guy. He taught me a lot about how to see the game a little different. How to kind of zoom out with the camera and see what the hitters are doing, what they're looking for. The way a swing might be leading to what they're sitting on. Things like that."

Zito was part of the A's Big Three starting rotation along with Tim Hudson and Mark Mulder. The rotation excelled in 2002 with Hudson winning 15 games, posting a 2.98 ERA (sixth best in the American League), and earning Player of the Week honors in mid-September. Mulder was the American League Pitcher of the Month in June and won 19 games.

"The three of us had different personalities," Zito says. "I was the California yoga surfer kid. Huddy was the Southern bulldog. And, Mulder was like the 6'6" drop-dead gorgeous pretty-boy stud athlete who could do anything. Like, me and Huddy used to call Mulder 'Cool Daddy-o.' Because Mulder was always too cool for us."

The three maintained a friendly competition and pushed each other to improve. And Zito loved watching Mulder pitch.

"That was probably the most enjoyable for me because he was throwing 92 miles-per-hour screwballs," Zito says. "People don't really understand what he used to do. He used to throw his fastball and pronate. The ball would come in at 92, and it was like a sinker nobody could get on top of. He would have 20 groundballs a game. So I used to love just watching Mulder do his thing."

Zito lived in the marina district in San Francisco. Before heading to the ballpark, he enjoyed spending time at his flat, playing guitar. He liked music because it was a release, a diversion from baseball where he didn't think about the next hitter he was facing or dwell on a less-than-favorable result from his prior start.

"I'd play guitar all day, and I'd go pitch. That year was great. I would go dominate; then I would come back and play guitar and just be like, 'This is really weird, man. I'm not stressing about the game. I'm just playing guitar. I go to work, kill it, and come back.' The self-conscious-ness of what's actually going on wasn't triggered yet."

During road trips, he brought his guitar.

"When I signed with the A's, I knew I was going to be in hotel rooms for so much time, so I wanted something to do. So I bought this guitar. The guitar just really helped me stay sane on the road."

He also liked to walk around and explore his neighborhood, going up and down Chestnut Street. He'd pop into a coffee shop or browse for CDs. Restaurants took him under their wings.

"I used to go to Judy's Café and Picaelli's Café." He smiles. "I'd get my little chicken sausage and avocado omelet with egg whites. Pat Pi-caelli, the owner, used to have the cooks make me football-size omelets. I used to eat those omelets on the days I was starting."

His game day routine started with the big breakfast around noon. He'd arrive at the park at 3:30 p.m. and, at 5:00, begin his process to prepare for the game, a routine he followed consistently.

"I'd get in the hot whirlpool for 15 minutes. Then I would shower, then I would get stretched out by the trainers, then I go get my uni on and get on the bike. Go through all my yoga stretches. Then I would go out to the field. Stretch again out there all over. Do my arm circles and tubing. Long toss. Bullpen. Yeah. It was very long. But it kept me in that place of focus."

On game days, Zito was serious. "I wasn't a guy that could be yuk-king it up with the guys and then just turn the switch. A lot of guys could do that. I couldn't."

His ideal mind-set was when he stood on the mound, saw the sign from Hernandez or Myers, and committed to that pitch. "At that point, what happens next—who cares? It's all about that one pitch. That's the ideal, anyway."

He liked pitching at home. "The Oakland Coliseum is one of my all-time favorite places to pitch. Just because it's so spread out. It's the most wide-open field now. I think a lot of them back in the day were like that, but now all these fields are geared to very small, kind of old-school, crowd-right-on-top-of-you kind of thing. The Coliseum is totally different. There's more foul territory there than probably three other fields combined."

In 2002, Zito was on such a roll that he didn't really talk shop with other pitchers to pick up tips of pitch sequences and strategies for facing hitters.

"I was just in that I'm-good-and-I-really-don't-know-why phase," he says. "It's unfortunate to say that, but I really embraced talking shop later in my career. When I really had to have an approach and a plan of this is what I'm doing instead of just like I'm nasty and just going out there."

In the midst of the success, Zito was named to the American League All-Star team. He pitched on the Sunday before the break in Kansas City, so he and his All-Star teammates, Miguel Tejada from the A's and Mike Sweeney from the Royals, chartered a private jet from Missouri to Milwaukee.

"We were big-time," he says with a grin.

Zito didn't expect to play in the game, having pitched two days prior. But as the game progressed and the American League had already used three pitchers, Joe Torre called Zito out of the bullpen to face Shawn Green leading off the bottom of the sixth inning.

"I remember coming in, and Robin Ventura was playing third," Zito says. "He came up to me to give me the ball, and I had pitched against him the year before. I was so nervous."

Zito looked at Ventura and said, "Dude, I'm more nervous than the playoffs right now."

Ventura wasn't a comforting, sympathetic listener. He tapped Zito on the ass and, stone-faced, said, "Go get 'em."

Today, Zito laughs. "He didn't give a shit."

Zito breathed deeply to face Green. Green hit a groundball to Tejada at shortstop, and Zito's 2002 All-Star Game experience was over after three pitches.

"Then [Eddie] Guardado came in, and then that whole shitstorm started, the whole tie game," Zito says, referring to the game, which, after nine innings, was tied at 7. After 11 innings and the score still knotted, the American League had used nine pitchers. The National League had used 10. With no other pitchers available, Commissioner Bud Selig, after consultation with Torre and National League manager Bob Brenly, declared the game over in a tie.

"Thank God it counts now," Zito says. "The Giants [in 2012]: We had home field advantage because of that whole rule."

Zito's success started attracting national attention. An independent thinker who was happy to do things his way, even if they were different compared to the mainstream (e.g., arm circles in the outfield as a crusty vet cursed him), Zito became the focus of stories about how he took satin pillowcases, aromatherapy candles, and stuffed animals with him on road trips. Zito says most of these stories are true. His mom read that pink satin helped alleviate acne. So he continued to sleep on pink satin pillowcases once he reached the big leagues. Some stories, though, were blown out of proportion. Before one interview, Zito staged his hotel room with an elaborate number of candles and animals.

"I didn't roll with 20 candles on a road trip," he says. "The interview, I put all this shit out."

## STREAKS

Three starts in July after the All-Star Game produced a 20 1/3 scoreless inning streak for Zito. During the same month, he also peeled off a string of five wins in a row.

But the 2002 Oakland A's owned the distinction of holding the American League's longest winning streak until the 2017 Indians won 22 games in a row. From August 13 through September 4, the A's won 20 straight games.

"It was magical at the end," Zito says. "We were down in most of those games. It might have even been game 20 . . . we were down 6–0 to the Royals, and we somehow came back. I don't even know how."

Fellow starting pitcher Cory Lidle was hot during the streak. "He pitched a game during that streak in Cleveland where he gave up a hit to the first hitter; then he retired the next 27," Zito says. "He was ridiculous!"

Zito also pitched exceptionally during the streak. For the 10th win, he pitched seven shutout innings against the Tigers. For win number 15, he threw five perfect innings against Kansas City.

"We were all hot at the same time," he says. "Looking back on it, I'm like, shit, man, going out every fifth day, I don't want to be the guy who screws this up. But I didn't have those thoughts. I was young and dumb and let's get after it. That's a beautiful thing, that innocence."

Zito credits the defense behind him as part of his and the team's success. Third baseman Eric Chavez won a Gold Glove. Shortstop Miguel Tejada won the Most Valuable Player Award, and Zito contends Tejada should have won a Gold Glove as well.

"Ron Washington single-handedly turned that kid into just an absolute force over there. I would watch a lot of these older games to remember what I did with three pitches—I put my cutter on the shelf before I came back last year [2015] and went back to fastball, curveball, change. I watched so many of these games from '01 and '02 and watching Miggy just do his thing. I was so blown away. That guy should have won multiple Gold Gloves over there."

Zito also praises the outfield.

"I was a fly-ball guy. So I needed good outfielders. Terrence Long was amazing out there chasing stuff down."

On September 13, Zito won his 21st game, beating Seattle. He had a no-hitter going into the eighth inning, but John Olerud led off with a single. Ruben Sierra followed with another hit.

"I just remember being so locked in," Zito says, thinking back on his no-hit bid. "I could put the ball anywhere I wanted. My curveball had so much depth, I think it looked like a fastball coming out to a lot of these guys, and I would have this huge break to it. I would go back and watch the tapes of that game in particular. Bret Boone taking a curveball for a strike, walking back to the dugout, kicking dirt, breaking his bat, snapping in the dugout."

He thinks back on the lineup he faced—Edgar Martinez, Ichiro Suzuki, John Olerud, Mike Cameron—and is amazed. "What a great team. I remember going out in that eighth inning and having that self-confidence thought of like, all right, man. Just keep it going. Well, all right. That's the end right there. John Olerud: jam shot base hit up the middle. Broke it up."

He worked hard throughout the season. On days in between starts, he adhered to strength coach Bob Alejo's regimen.

"Through the course of that year, we were trying to get up to 1,000 pounds on leg press, and I remember I got to 1,000 in Detroit. That was a big day for me."

Zito laughs. "It's so funny how different I am now. I wouldn't even get near a leg press at the end of my career, you know?"

He mixed upper and lower body conditioning. Because of an injury to one of his knees, he didn't run. He rode a stationary bike instead. On his second and third days in between starts, he used an unorthodox approach and pitched two bullpen sessions, each 30 to 35 pitches where he concentrated on repeating and maintaining his delivery.

"That's unheard of these days," he says. "Everyone is terrified of people blowing out, so they think less is more. I always thought more is more, throwingwise. I would throw a 35-to-40-pitch bullpen on day two and day three, and then get a day off and pitch again."

## PLAYOFFS

The 20-game winning streak propelled the A's from third place to first in the American League West Division and clinched a return appearance in the postseason, this time facing the Minnesota Twins in the first-round American League Division Series. The teams split the first two games in Oakland before traveling to Minneapolis where Art Howe asked Zito to start Game Three in the Hubert H. Humphrey Metrodome.

"The thing that stands out in my head more than anything about that game was how loud it was," he says. "I remember they said the Who, the loudest band, performs at like 112 decibels. And I think they measured in [the Metrodome] like 118. It was something crazy."

The team had banners of Twins greats like Harmon Killebrew, Kirby Puckett, and Kent Hrbek covering some seats. To increase capacity by another 4,000 or 5,000 for the playoffs, they removed these. The result? Fifty thousand people waving white rally towels.

"That place was louder than two Yankee Stadiums," Zito says.

The dome grew so loud that it looked like catcher Ramon Hernandez's fingers were shaking when he put down the signs.

"The only way I can explain it is that the sound waves were bouncing off of me to the point where my eyes couldn't, like [focus]. I don't even know if that's possible. But I was having a very difficult time. It was so loud."

He describes the sound as so overwhelming that, even with catcher Hernandez standing next to him and yelling, Zito still couldn't hear him. Because of the increased noise, Rick Peterson suggested that Zito wear earplugs. He tried them during his bullpen session, but they felt uncomfortable, so he opted not to use them for the game.

The game started with an inside-the-park home run by the A's Ray Durham. In the bottom of the first, A's first baseman Scott Hatteberg lost a fly ball in the Metrodome's white ceiling. Later, Zito stepped back into his windup to throw a curveball, and the ball slipped out and traveled only 12 feet.

"I would always hold the ball real loose. They would say hold it like an egg. And it came out behind me during my windup."

Zito earned the win, pitching six innings and holding the Twins to three runs, but the A's lost the next two games and the series. Minnesota advanced to face the Angels, and the A's season when they won 103 games was over.

## INDIVIDUAL ACHIEVEMENT

Shortly after the season ended, Zito learned he won the Cy Young Award, beating out Red Sox Pedro Martinez and Derek Lowe.

"It was pretty surreal," he says. "I was dating a girl in San Francisco. We were just having a lazy morning at her place, and I got a call from my agent at the time, Joel Wolfe. Back then, they didn't wait until the end of the playoffs or the World Series to announce. They just did it a couple of days after the season. So, he called me one morning. I picked up the phone. He's like, 'Well, you won the Cy Young Award.'"

"Holy shit!" Zito said. "That's crazy!"

Zito appeared at a press conference to discuss winning the award. His picture was on the front page of the *San Francisco Chronicle* the next day. So, as Zito stood in line at a Southwest Airlines terminal to fly home to LA, the attendant at the desk kept looking at his newspaper and the 6-foot-2 pitcher waiting to board.

"Hey, Barry," the Southwest employee said. "Why don't you pre-board?"

Zito smiles now. "So I got to preboard that day. Because my face was on the cover of the *Chronicle*."

Sandy Koufax presented Zito with the award.

"We were talking out in the hall, and we were going back to our rooms after the event," Zito says. "He was telling me how to throw the curveball, to pull down on the second finger. I was like, wow! That's awesome."

Zito started doing some acting, playing himself in an episode of *The Chris Isaak Show* and appearing in *JAG* ("That was real acting."). He was having fun, but he says his ego was growing to extremes.

"My ego was so out of check," Zito says. "I wanted to be on every TV show. I wanted to be on the radio. A lot of that stuff went to my head."

Zito continued to pitch well, well enough to attract the interest of the San Francisco Giants when he became a free agent in 2006; the team signed him to one of the richest contracts in baseball: seven years for $126 million.

"I had the highest highs and the lowest lows in San Francisco," he says. "I mean, the lowest low was 2010. I got left off the [postseason] roster. I got brought over there. I got paid the highest contract in the game ever for a pitcher, to go over there and win a World Series and be the face of the franchise. And struggled. Didn't have a terrible year in '07 . . . '08 was a terrible year . . . '09 was decent . . . 2010, I started out great, and then I tanked at the end of the year, so they left me off the roster because they took their four top pitchers."

Making this 2010 postseason low even lower was Zito's father Joe suffering a stroke four days after Zito learned he wasn't going to the playoffs. Zito was stressed, traveling back and forth to Los Angeles to be with his dad and join his team to support them.

"I was a wreck, man," he says.

Once again, Zito found solace in music.

"I'd come home at night and play guitar and try to write music until 3:00 a.m. And I'd just drive around. I lived in San Francisco at the time, lived in the marina [district]. I would drive my car around in the different neighborhoods and listen to music."

But in 2012, Zito experienced success on the mound again. He went back to the basics and recalled lessons Randy Jones taught him as a teenager, calling him lefty and spitting toward his feet to get his attention.

"After the front foot was the number one thing he would tell me," Zito says. "Whip down after your foot, which sounds very simple, but it's hilarious because, at the end of my career, really focusing on what it felt like to release the baseball, that this is the fulcrum, and this is the thing that you're trying to speed up, that relationship was everything that led to my success in the playoffs in 2012."

Zito won 15 games and beat Justin Verlander in Game One of the World Series.

"All that stuff was just storybook," Zito says. "I think that was God just saying, 'Hey, man. You can still show your face in San Francisco! You can come back here and not get yelled at, not get bottles broken on your head.' So I'm grateful for that."

Zito learned a lot about himself while he wore a Giants uniform.

"It just really made me who I am today. It gave me a sense of humility I never would have had if I didn't struggle over there the way I did. And I'm grateful for that. As much as I would still love to be playing now and love to have a Hall of Fame–caliber career, being the person I am now with peace in my heart and humility, I think, wow. I'm so grateful for everything that happened."

Zito credits finding Christianity in 2011 as the basis for his peace and his outlook grounded in gratitude.

"It changed everything for me," he says. "Not so much on the field but as far as who I am and the level of acceptance I have for who I am instead of trying to be someone else. I mean, I battle it every day still, but I'm much more of a grateful person now instead of an entitled person. I can talk about my past failures and laugh now whereas before you would never find me laughing about anything where I struggled."

Looking back, he remembers the articles from 2002 wherein he stated he had figured out a way to find the zone, and he shakes his head.

"I didn't figure shit out," he says. "If I figured it out, I would've won a few more Cy Youngs and probably been in the Hall of Fame. That was a young kid who thought he figured it out. And baseball humbled him like it has most people."

Today, the lessons of focus Zito would try to impart to other pitchers is to turn your head off. "Stay in the present moment. Stay in your body. Live as moment to moment as you possibly can. You know, all those crazy zen things. That's not bullshit. Get into your senses. Because they say the second you're aware of being in the zone, you're not in the zone anymore. You can't access it on purpose. It's such an evasive thing."

## THE NEXT VERSE

In 2013, the Giants elected not to pick up Zito's option to return for the 2014 season. Zito resented the move.

"I had struggled," Zito says. "I was in the bullpen for half of that season. And man, I was making pitches. Felt good about how I was throwing, and they were just whacking it. And that was the first time in my career that, after the game, I was like, I actually feel good about what I did except I gave up six runs."

Zito took a year off and trained by himself. He wanted to come back on his terms and walk away on his terms. Not for his father or anybody else—for himself.

"I didn't want to walk off bitter."

The Oakland A's brought Zito to spring training in 2015. They liked what they saw but not well enough to place him on the major-league roster. They told him he could pitch for their Triple-A team in Nashville.

"What a blessing," he says. "I fell in love with baseball again."

And he was in a town that is a natural fit for the next chapter in Zito's life: writing songs and pursuing a career in music.

"I was in LA for 15 years. I used to fly the flag for LA, and my wife did too. I just loved being in LA with the ambition and the creativity and the risk taking, getting outside of your comfort zone. Here, you have a lot of that, but you also have the family values. You have the God factor here."

As the 2015 season ended, Zito took the mound one last time, a start in Anaheim against the Angels, the team he faced for his first big-league start 15 years earlier. He pitched four innings, and mission accomplished. He walked away on his own terms.

Looking back nearly 15 years after winning the Cy Young Award, Zito is pleased to be a part of the pitching elite fraternity.

"I don't think I was as grateful for what it was back then," he says. "I was expecting to win more and more of those, and that didn't happen."

Zito's award hangs in his studio, underneath a champagne bottle from the 2012 World Series celebration he framed. When he's tying ends of a songwriting tale together or searching for the right chord, he can look up to a symbol of excellence for positive memories and inspiration. Because, after all, Zito says he was in a good space in 2002.

"What makes that year different for me versus every other year is that there was probably more self-trust on a day-to-day basis. Which stemmed from having a great time. It's like that thing: When you're relaxed, you're going to do your best."

He pauses.

"When guys can be themselves, they're going to perform their best. I felt more free to be myself that year. That year and the last three months of 2012 were probably when I felt most liberated to be who I was."

In 2016, Zito spends his days on Music Row with other songwriters, sharing ideas and writing songs, searching for the next radio hit. He gathers his four or five best tunes, and studio musicians record them. He steps to a microphone and sings the vocals, and he has a product he pitches to artists, managers, and producers. He's also taking piano lessons and learning how the recording program Pro Tools works.

"My long-term goal is to write and produce artists, my own stuff, just to do everything. Be a one-stop shop basically."

In addition, Zito continues public service work. During his playing days, he formed a nonprofit to provide assistance to veterans and their families. In 2016, Zito partnered with the Easter Seals to continue this work on a larger scale, with the goal of providing more grants to veterans for medical care and to cover expenses for family members as they travel to spend time with their loved ones as they recuperate.

The song continues—from pitching artistry to songwriting craftsmanship to doing what he can to make the world a better place.

World champions and the best at his craft: champagne and Zito's Cy Young
Award. Courtesy of Barry Zito.

# 9

# CLIMB THE MOUNTAIN: R. A. DICKEY

## 2012 NATIONAL LEAGUE CY YOUNG AWARD

*I met R. A. Dickey at the Chile Burrito restaurant in Brentwood, Tennessee, on a Friday afternoon to talk. Most of the conversation focused on the knuckleball and how Dickey fine-tuned baseball's most unpredictable pitch, but we also discussed books, writing, and self-discovery. With his dark hair easing toward the longish side and beard, Dickey looked the same as he did when the media took note of the articulate veteran with an unconventional pitch emerging as the ace of the New York Mets pitching staff. Born and raised in Nashville, Dickey speaks with a Southern lilt, and, after I lived in the South for 20 years but recently relocated to Oklahoma, the accent reminded me of home. We began our conversation by discussing writing, with Dickey sharing his process for writing his memoir,* Wherever I Wind Up, *published just as the 2012 season opened: "I had journal entries going back to my seventh-grade year. So, I was able to pull off those, and I would write. I would write 2,500 words, send it to Wayne [Coffey, his coauthor], he'd edit and shape it, we'd talk about it, then he did a bunch of interviews about some things he thought would be interesting to put in there, and then he'd write 2,500 words, and we'd look over it and edit together. So, there wasn't a word that didn't come through my purview, right? It was all a collaboration, but I wanted to write my own book. I did not want him to write it."* [1]

By the end of the 2011 season, R. A. Dickey had climbed a lot of mountains, figuratively. He had reached the big leagues and was achieving consistent success. Off the field, he was concentrating on being a better husband and father. To do that, he worked with a therapist and unflinchingly confronted emotional wounds from his past. He was also putting the finishing touches on a manuscript about his life's journey, a marathon challenge in itself. On top of all that, he was, in fact, preparing to climb a mountain—Mount Kilimanjaro in Tanzania, Africa.

Dickey pursued these lofty endeavors with one foot forward at a time, each step moving a little closer to another peak, be it improving his knuckleball, being more attentive and in the moment with his family, honing his memoir, or preparing for the high altitudes halfway across the world from his home in Nashville. For his physical climb, once the 2011 season ended and he was back home, Dickey strapped on a heavy backpack and an oxygen deprivation mask and ran, preferably in the cold and at night, so he would be ready for the mountain's demands. The climb would be rewarding, reaching the peak and seeing stunning views and feeling the satisfaction of accomplishing a hard-earned goal while knowing all the training and sacrifice it took to summit. This would most definitely be an individual accomplishment to be proud of, but Dickey would also find satisfaction in knowing the expedition was raising money to build a medical clinic in Kamathipura, India, the red-light district in Mumbai. The area teemed with prostitutes lured to the city from their villages with the promise that they could earn money by cleaning office buildings and send the money back home to their families. Once they arrived in the city, though, there were no office buildings to clean, just prostitution and rampant HIV.

"These prostitutes would come and be treated for free at this place, and we would get a chance to hear their stories. It was kind of an entry point to rescuing them away from that life," Dickey says. "Once you've built up a relationship with these women, you say, hey, there's a different way to live if you're interested in that."

Dickey's climb raised $250,000 to build the clinic. He spent two weeks in January hiking the switchbacks, climbing Kilimanjaro, and reaching two summits. The conditioning and climbing left him in the best shape of his life when he reported to spring training in Port St. Lucie, Florida, in February 2012, a 37-year-old man beginning his 17th season of professional baseball, continuing his climb with more peaks waiting.


## GETTING TO 2012

Dickey began his professional career as a conventional pitcher, relying on his fastball and changing speed and location. After eight seasons with the Texas Rangers organization, Dickey had appeared in 67 big-league games, bouncing from the Rangers to one of their minor-league affiliates, usually the Triple-A Oklahoma RedHawks, and back, when Rangers manager Buck Showalter and pitching coach (and 1988 National League Cy Young Award winner) Orel Hershiser suggested Dickey try something different and become a knuckleball pitcher.[2] In 2005, Dickey worked with mentor Charlie Hough, who had spent 25 years in the major leagues tossing knucklers and winning 216 games along the way. Dickey also sought help from Hall of Fame knuckleballer Phil Niekro as well as from Tim Wakefield, a former first baseman who was on his way out of baseball when he began throwing knuckleballs to reinvent himself as a big-league starter for 19 seasons. But mastering the knuckleball wasn't as simple as learning a grip and *presto!* having a new pitch. The release was different. The mechanics were different. The mind-set was different, forcing Dickey to relearn pitching while also carrying a new role or label: pitching oddity.

"You're always battling this, that-guy's-a-circus-freak kind of thing with that pitch. You're always behind that," he says. "If you were to have a crappy two or three months as a knuckleballer, everybody's 'I told you so!' As a conventional pitcher, they don't say that, but as a knuckleballer, it's like, 'That was bound to happen. There's no legitimacy to what he's doing. It's a trick. Smoke and mirrors.' And what they don't understand is that it's so much harder than being a conventional pitcher."

As an illustration, Dickey points to the relative certainty a conventional pitcher has knowing where each pitch is going. If he throws 15 two-seam fastballs, the pitcher knows 95 percent of the time what the ball's movement will be. If he throws 15 curveballs, he knows where each will be and how it will move. Fifteen knuckleballs? They will all be different.

"I had to get to this place with that pitch where the only thing I could take care of was the mechanics before I distributed the pitch and the release point and that was it. After that, I had to kind of surrender to what it was going to do," Dickey says. "It was a lesson in how to surrender well. And be out of control, which is hard. Because you want to be in control so much. As a pitcher, we're taught control our whole lives. And then, with this pitch, you can't do that."

Sometimes, those moments of surrender produce a fluttering and unhittable pitch. And it's a beautiful thing to see from the mound as it travels to the plate. When Dickey executed the pitch optimally, the ball popped from his hand, his pointer and middle fingers dug into the leather behind the horseshoe seams, his thumb and ring finger balancing the ball on the sides. Careful not to push the ball with his fingers (pushing would create spin, which knuckleballers want to avoid at all costs), the gravity of his pitching motion enabled the ball to slide from his hand moving forward with as little rotation as possible. After releasing a good knuckleball, the ball looked like a pool cue moving toward home plate, with no red seams spinning to interrupt the monochromatic white.

"I'm just letting the velocity of my arm take the ball out of my hand," Dickey says. "And when it does that right, you can hear it. It's like a whisper."

When the knuckleball works, it confounds hitters. But when the pitch doesn't flutter, things can go badly for a knuckleballer.

"You have to learn to swallow how bad this pitch can be," Dickey says. "When it's ugly, it's super ugly. People are chasing it to the backstop every two seconds or walking guys. People are stealing bases all around you. It's just ugly."

Despite the disappointing and trying episodes, knuckleballers must remain committed to the pitch.

"You've got to be able to swallow [those instances when the pitch is bad] and wake up the next day and say I'm still meant to be a knuckleballer," Dickey says. "It plays tricks on your mind in ways that being a conventional pitcher never did. Like, I wake up the next day as a conventional pitcher—okay, I just didn't have a good day. I'll go back, and I'll do better. With a knuckleball, you're like, 'Have I lost it? Do I know how to do it?' It starts messing with you, man. So, you've got to have the

**"It's like a whisper." R. A. Dickey gripping the knuckleball. Author's collection.**

mental fortitude to say, bullshit. It's good. Even though you had a bad outing."

Dickey achieved that fortitude.

"My whole mentality was centered around how do I be consistent with an inconsistent pitch," he says. "I was a knuckleballer. The very nature of the pitch is based on inconsistencies, right? The movement, the lateness of the movement, the speed of the pitch—there's so many different variables that can occur over the flight of the pitch, and I had to figure out a way to wrestle with that and produce a trustworthy product that my general manager and manager could say, okay, here's a guy who we can trust when we put him out there to throw strikes to control the game. And that's all I cared about. That was my expectation. I would say that my expectation was really reduced down to trying to live incrementally the next five minutes well. How do I do that, over and over and over again throughout a day?"

That's where Dickey's headspace as a pitcher was going into the 2012 season. He anticipated a good year. Beginning in 2010, he had more command of the knuckleball, and he was having success with the Mets, quietly staying under the radar while piling up solid outings. In 2010, he made 26 starts, won 11 games, and maintained a 2.84 ERA. The next season, he made 32 starts, threw 208 2/3 innings, and had a tidy 3.28 ERA.

As a person, Dickey was in a good place too. In April, his memoir *Wherever I Wind Up* was published. In the book, he reflects on growing up in a broken home, the victim of sexual abuse; discovering passions for reading, writing, and baseball; and achieving a dream when the Texas Rangers selected him in the first round of the 1996 draft. Then physicians discovered an abnormality in Dickey's elbow, an abnormality that caused the Rangers to rescind their offer. A huge detour for Dickey, but, resilient, he accepted the Rangers' invitation to join their organization albeit at a much lower contract amount. Dickey was up and down between the Rangers and their Triple-A affiliate until Showalter and Hershiser encouraged him to explore the knuckleball. Dickey made gradual progress with the new pitch as he moved to the Milwaukee Brewers, Seattle Mariners, and Minnesota Twins organizations over the next three seasons. He also made some discoveries about himself— acknowledging and working through the scars of sexual abuse and shifting his focus from defining his worth in terms of successful games on a baseball diamond to becoming a better husband and father.

"When I figured out a lot of my identity as a human being was tied up in my performance as a baseball player, and I kind of arrived at the place where I felt like if I was going to have any success at all, I needed to change," Dickey says. "And it's kind of counterintuitive, right? You feel you've got to be 100 percent in and not having room for anything else in your life, but I found that not to be the case as I started to grow as a human being, right? I found that the more I really got my validation from things that were worthwhile and long term, the baseball stuff was kind of just an overflow. It didn't define me. And, because it didn't define me, I was able to rebound from tough outings easier. And I was able to hold great outings where they should be and not be consumed by ego, you know? It was the thing that transformed my career was how to do that dance differently. Because most players, that's how they have had validation their whole life. And so, when that starts to fall apart, if they don't have any real foundational things that they're about, they crumble, and that's it. They end up having horror stories once they get out of the game. It's sad. So that was big for me, figuring that out while I was still playing, and it kind of coincided with the 2010, '11, '12 seasons. I was doing a lot of work on myself here locally with a great therapist and really learning how to live differently, and that was very helpful. So once I started to apply some of the things I learned, it wasn't about how much I prepared as much as the six inches between my ears."

Sports Illustrated published an excerpt from Dickey's book on April 2. Dickey was worried how teammates would react.

"It was one of the more intimate excerpts from the book, and I remember before I walked in [the clubhouse] thinking that I was going to be alienated in some regards because I was sharing such sensitive material. And I remember thinking my teammates were not going to know what to do with that, but I had a lot of great response from that, which was a real encouragement to me."

## HOT BEGINNING

Once the regular season began, Dickey raced to an excellent start. By the All-Star break, he was 12–1 with a 2.40 ERA, 123 strikeouts, and only 26 walks, a significant statistic for an unpredictable pitch. Two wins were consecutive one-hitters when he struck out 12 and 13 batters, respectively. Amid the success, he set a Mets record for consecutive scoreless innings (32 2/3).

Dickey attributes the success to consistent and good mechanics achieved through a routine of work and repetition.

"I was like a robot out there. Every position of every body part was in the right place. I felt like in order to produce what I needed to produce from a knuckleball standpoint, my ideal knuckleball was one-half of a revolution from the time it left my hand to the time it got to home plate. That was all I could really allow for, for it to be what I considered ideal. A quarter revolution to a half revolution. And I just was able to throw one after the other that would do that. My mechanics were just right. I was really confident. I had a great routine going in between starts."

Dickey's routine following a start was to have a day of rest. The next day, he pitched a bullpen with his regular catcher, Josh Thole.

"The pen would always be before batting practice when nobody was out there, and I could really get the work I needed to do done, and I was very deliberate about that. I remember that being very helpful to me," Dickey says. "I really depended on that routine. I was never a guy who could just kind of say, aw, I'll get to it whenever or if I miss one, it's okay. I was probably annoying with how regimented I needed to be and felt like I needed to be."

A contrast to conventional pitchers, Dickey threw his bullpens at full speed, 60 to 80 pitches. Part of this is attributable to his throwing the knuckleball as his primary pitch—he's not throwing as hard as a fastball and curveball pitcher, so he can throw at full speed more. But it also goes back to feel and command of the pitch.

"I didn't want to over and over repeat what it was like to throw a 60-, 70-mile-an-hour knuckleball, and I was going to be throwing 80-mile-an-hour knuckleballs in the game."

During these sessions, Dickey anticipated the next lineup he was facing, and he worked through pitch sequences. With a batter standing in the box, Dickey envisioned the leadoff hitter he would face in his next game, and he worked through the data—is he a first-pitch swinger? Does he like high or low pitches? Does he take first pitches? Analyzing and bringing the information together, Dickey tailored his pitch selection and sequence. He would throw two hard knuckleballs followed by a slow one. Fine-tuning the pressure he applied with his fingertips to make the ball move, he threw a pitch breaking at a batter's feet followed by one sweeping away. ("It was microscience out there," Dickey says.) Then pitching coach Dan Warthen would chime in, "Now would be a good time to throw him a fastball. He's seen six knuckleballs in a row. And that'll open up your changeup for the next time through the lineup." Dickey would mix one in and move on to the next hitter in the upcoming lineup.

"When I threw a bullpen, I didn't just practice getting my arm loose. I had some intentionality behind it on how I wanted to work guys," Dickey says. "I would have a guy stand in to be Bryce Harper and Jayson Werth and Freddie Freeman, and so, when I got to that spot in the game, I had already faced those guys. So, psychologically, I knew right where to go."

These practice sessions of envisioning pitching to a team's best hitter helped during game situations.

"You felt like you had already worked a guy," Dickey says. "It was no surprise when there was second and third and one out and shit was hitting the fan—you didn't have to panic. Because, okay, I've worked this sequence with David Ortiz already. This is what I'm going to do, and I'm going to execute it. You have this kind of unnamed confidence when you do things like that."

Dickey adopted this approach when he became a knuckleballer. He really embraced it during 2010, and he followed it through the rest of his baseball career.

"I just felt like I needed it with that pitch," he says. "It was such a feel pitch. When it comes out of your hand, you know it's a great knuckleball as soon as it leaves your fingertips."

Dickey had to train judiciously. He played most of 2012 with a strained oblique muscle, which meant he couldn't work out as hard or as much as he wanted to. He had to prioritize how he used his body to prepare for games, and he devoted his resources to bullpens.

On days he started, he arrived at the park early. He ate a meal and then watched film of a prior outing against the team he was facing, with either Dickey or Tim Wakefield as the pitcher. He reviewed charts for insights—who liked first-pitch fastballs? Who stole bases? Fifty minutes before game time, Dickey began a routine, taking a shower, putting his uniform on, and going to the workout room. He turned on some blue-grass or Journey or *Monster Ballads* and hopped on the stationary bicy-cle to get his blood flowing. He mixed in some push-ups and body squats. With a little sweat on his brow, he moved to the field, and, 25 minutes before game time, he played long toss for eight minutes, gradu-ally moving closer until 70 feet separated Dickey and his catcher. Then he stepped to the bullpen's mound and threw three fastballs down the middle, three fastballs away, three fastballs in. Then, three changeups, right in the middle of the plate. If he was throwing a breaking ball, he threw three of those, also in the middle of the plate. Then he threw 20 knuckleballs, and, like his practice bullpen sessions in between games, he envisioned the lineup he was preparing to face.

Then it was time to take the ball and step on the mound and compete.

Though Dickey was on a roll, it wasn't until his 11th start, a game against St. Louis at Citi Field, the game immediately following the first no-hitter in Mets history, that he thought the 2012 season might be special for him. Dickey threw a seven-hit shutout, striking out nine. Midgame with runners on second and third, he threw a borderline strike knuckleball to Matt Holliday at a 1–2 count. The umpire gave Dickey the benefit of the doubt, and the strikeout pulled Dickey out of a jam.

"That changed the whole trajectory of the game," Dickey says.

He also threw a hanging knuckleball to Carlos Beltran at the end of the game. Beltran's swing made Dickey think the ball would land seven rows past the fence. But Beltran hit the ball off the end of the bat, and the bomb became a fly ball to right field.

In this same game, Dickey also discovered a high knuckleball. He threw it by shortening his stride and dropping his elbow slightly. He liked how the ball moved, toppling down at home plate, its late movement frazzling hitters. He liked it so well that he concentrated his next bullpen session on fine-tuning the pitch. And he continued to use the high knuckleball for the remainder of the season.

By the All-Star break, Dickey had the best record in the National League, and he anticipated starting the game. But manager Tony LaRussa pulled Dickey aside the day before the game and told him he was rewarding Matt Cain for his body of work and starting him.

"That's fine," Dickey said.

With the game counting for home-field advantage in the World Series, LaRussa was concerned with catcher Buster Posey, who had never caught a knuckleball, thrust into working with Dickey. Nonetheless, Dickey had a fine All-Star experience. In the bottom of the sixth, he gave up a single to Mike Trout. He struck out Mark Trumbo. He hit Paul Konerko with a pitch, and Miguel Cabrera hit into a double play to end the inning.

Dickey enjoyed the All-Star experience with his family joining him in Kansas City for the festivities. But it was a whirlwind experience, and Dickey was soon flying back to New York to appear on the *Late Show with David Letterman*. Letterman plugged Dickey's book. And he asked to catch a knuckleball.

"Don't throw them full speed, okay?" Letterman said.

"I won't," Dickey said. "Are you wearing a cup?"

"No."

"Well, you might want to turn your body a little."

## KEYS TO SUCCESS

Looking back on 2012, Dickey points to several aspects that made the season a successful and special one for him.

One factor was his manager Terry Collins, who took over in 2011, Dickey's second season with the team. Although some managers are skeptical of knuckleballers and their erratic pitch, Collins trusted Dickey and treated him respectfully as a professional devoted to his craft.

"Terry for me was probably if not the best, one of the best two managers I've ever had. And the reason was because he was an incredible communicator, and he trusted me," Dickey says. "And that is a rarity in that industry to have a relationship with a manager where you can be honest with him without being judged or feeling like he doesn't have your best interests at hand. He's paid to help us win games; I'm paid to help us win games; and we can cut through the macho bravado bullcrap and do that well together."

To illustrate, Dickey says that, after six or seven innings, if he felt like he didn't have a great feel for the ball leaving his hand, he didn't try to play the hero and soldier on and finish the game. He could tell Collins he might want to consider getting someone up in the bullpen to come into the game in relief. And their communication and trust in each other typically resulted in the reliever saving the game for a win. Likewise, if Dickey scuffled early and gave up a few runs and Collins approached him in the fourth or fifth inning and asked how he was feeling, Collins listened when Dickey assured him that he had found his feel and was rolling. Collins would leave Dickey in the game, and the result would usually be a win.

"When you have that kind of relationship, one, it's very rare," Dickey says. "Because the manager wants to be in charge. But when it comes to a knuckleball and managing a knuckleballer, it's a whole different world than managing a conventional pitcher. Because the pitch can come and go over the course of a game. Maybe three or four times. So, if you have a good, open line of communication, and I was older in my career, so I wasn't afraid to tell the truth. When you're young, so many things get in the way. You don't want to be perceived in a certain way or act like you don't want to take the ball. I didn't care about any of that. I just wanted to win. Do well and contribute. So, if I wasn't feeling great, even though the scoreboard read zero, I would tell him. And I would also tell him if I thought he shouldn't take me out. And he listened. That doesn't happen often. And that was probably one of the reasons that I was able to thrive under his leadership so well."

Dickey believes his relationship with Collins was so good because Collins could see how dedicated Dickey was.

"He knew how much work I had put in," Dickey says. "He knew I was older. And frankly, he was receptive to that kind of relationship. You can't have that with everybody, and I think that he enjoyed that part of it as much as I did. It's refreshing when you can tell the truth, and it'd be okay. He created a culture where that was okay for me and vice versa. So, we just really worked well together."

Dickey also enjoyed working with catcher Josh Thole, who caught 26 of Dickey's 33 starts in 2012. The two had a history going back to spring training 2010 as batterymates, both of them on the cusp of making the Mets roster.

"I was in major-league camp, but I knew I probably wasn't going to make the team, and he was catching me when he got sent down in the Triple-A games," Dickey says. "He had never caught me. My first 10 knuckleballs, I bet two of them hit leather. The other ones were either off his mask or shin guard."

From that moment forward, Thole spent a lot of time with Dickey, catching a bullpen or catching Dickey in the outfield. Time working together built trust and confidence.

"I knew he could catch my best knuckleball," Dickey says. "A lot of catchers, they'll catch your good ones, but they're not going to catch your best ones. And a lot of times, your best ones are with runners in scoring position or with two strikes, and, if he drops it, that guy's running to first. Or, there's a guy on third and you throw your bastard knuckleball, and he can't catch it? Well, that guy's scoring. I didn't have to worry about that with Josh. I mean, yes, he had some passed balls, but he was so good back there. I didn't have to worry about him."

Thole remembers one game catching Dickey. Things weren't clicking. Dickey had given up some hits. Baserunners were on. Before the situation got out of hand, Thole lifted his mask and jogged out to the mound to talk to Dickey. But . . .

"What do you tell a knuckleballer?" Thole says.[3]

Thole arrived at the mound. Dickey stared at him, perturbed. Dickey liked to work quickly, and the visit disrupted his rhythm.

Thole stared back. He still didn't know what to say, but he offered, "Just make the ball move more, I guess."[4]

"Go back to home plate," Dickey said.[5]

Thole turned around and trotted back to the plate and set up. Dickey retired the next hitter and was out of the jam.

Dickey had also mastered pitch selection and relied on the resources he used as a conventional pitcher, mixing them in at the right moments. As an example, he points to throwing a first-pitch fastball during his first trip through the lineup.

"Most hitters, first time through the lineup, they don't want to swing at a first-pitch knuckleball," Dickey says. "They want to see how it's going to behave. They want to get a look and know what it does. So, I would pump a first-pitch heater in there, and they would take it, and it'd be 83, right down the middle. Strike one. So, now I'm ahead in the count, and I haven't even shown them my best pitch."

Dickey recognized he couldn't start all at-bats off with a first-pitch fastball. So, for variety, for the second time through the lineup, his first pitch was a changeup, 11 miles an hour slower than his fastball. Batters would be so far ahead of the pitch, "they'd screw themselves in the ground," Dickey says. "And, so, once I figured out the psychology of how to do that better, that was big for me."

Dickey also perfected fingernail maintenance. To grip the knuckleball, the length of Dickey's pointer and middle fingernails needed to be precise. He used a glass file—two strokes meant 1/16 of a centimeter removed. Early in the season when the colder weather made his nails more brittle and susceptible to breaking, he applied nail hardener.

The bottom line: Things clicked for Dickey in 2012.

"It was just one of those years, man. It was a Cy Young year. I was doing whatever I wanted with the knuckleball. I was changing height levels. I was changing breaks. I was changing speeds. I was throwing it for strikes," he says. "The thing that was uncanny about that year was how many walks I had. I think I averaged barely two walks per nine innings, and I don't say that to boast. I say that just because that was what was different. I just wasn't walking anybody."

## UNPREDICTABILITY WITH AN EXPONENT

While each knuckleball has its own chaotic movement, Dickey created more unpredictability by changing speeds. He threw the pitch harder than most knuckleballers, between 78 and 81 miles per hour. But by shortening his stride toward to the plate, he slowed the pitch down significantly. And he fooled batters. His arm speed was the same, and, with their eyes on the ball and not on his feet, they couldn't deduce that Dickey was setting the pitch up to travel slower.

Dickey attributes his finding different knuckleball options to being curious and trying new things.

"I think one of the things that's so special about life is to try to be a lifelong learner," he says. "I always kind of had that mentality. And have people around me that coach that in me, to be a lifelong learner. Don't ever think that you've got all the answers. So, that helped me, trying to learn, trying to adapt, asking questions, being curious."

He also acknowledges that, for him to be successful, he had to be creative.

"I didn't have the luxury of being Doc Gooden," Dickey says. "I was not blessed with what some of those, Tom Seaver and some of those guys were blessed with, just raw, unadulterated talent. Where they could just throw their jocks on the field and strike out 25 guys. I couldn't do that. I had to find a different way."

In terms of the knuckleball's movement, where Dickey pitched played a role in how the ball traveled from his hand to the catcher's glove. Although his 2012 record indicates equal success at home and on the road (at Citi Field: 10–3, 2.59 ERA, three complete games, two shutouts, 116 strikeouts, and *only* 30 walks; away: 10–3, 2.90 ERA, two complete games, one shutout, 114 strikeouts, and *only* 24 walks), he loved pitching at Citi Field because of its spacious dimensions as well as its humidity and the way the wind usually blew slightly toward the pitcher, factors that helped make knuckleballs knuckle.

"Anytime you have wind resistance against a nonrotating object, it's going to create more chaos," Dickey says. "The speed of the wind resisting the baseball contributes to how well it moves. So, that was good for me. The wind behind me was horrible. If it pushed to the plate, even though [as a conventional pitcher] you would beg for that, as a knuckleballer, I did not like it. Because it moves the ball towards the hitter before it could really break as many times as I wanted it to. Even when I threw great ones, those became kind of mediocre ones because the wind was pushing it to the plate before it could really do its stuff."

On the road, he liked pitching in Tampa Bay and in Toronto, domes with air-conditioning units that created the desired air movement of a slight breeze blowing in Dickey's face.

Parks not as conducive to the knuckleball: Colorado and Arizona. The combination of thin air, no humidity, and no circulation made it more difficult for the knuckleball to break. Dickey had to adapt and throw hard knuckleballs most of the game to create more air resistance instead of varying the pitch with different speeds.

## PERSPECTIVE

Dickey was consistently excellent throughout 2012, but, if he had a game he wasn't pleased with, he had a couple of ways he dealt with a setback to learn from it and move on.

"Greg Maddux told me something later in my career that made a lot of sense to me. He said any good pitcher has to have a bulletproof confidence and a short-term memory. And so, I kind of feel like that was one of the ways I dealt with it was, grieving it for a moment but just really trying to use and be self-aware of about what had happened in the game to try to get better," Dickey says. "You have to be able to manage failure if you're going to be an athlete. It just doesn't go your way all the time."

Sometimes, Dickey would take a rough outing and wash it down the drain. Literally.

"Immediately, the way I would do it is I would take a shower. Every bad game I ever had, I'd go in, sometimes with all my uniform on and just soak in the shower and take my uniform off and put it in the hamper, and like, that was the end of it. Like, that was the way I could physically turn the page. It was almost like a physical representation of what I wanted my mentality to be. Like, okay. Think through while I'm in the shower, let the water wash it all away, and then start over the next day. That was something that worked for me."

He would also call his wife Anne and talk about the game. He journaled regularly. ("It was therapeutic for me. It helped me a lot. So, if I'd had a bad game, I'd write about it.")

"If you let one outing spiral into the next, you're in trouble," he says. "So much of being a good athlete I felt like was how do you arrest that free fall and change the trajectory. That's a mechanism I work very hard to try to develop. And I certainly didn't get it perfect, but I felt like I had a good routine when it came to dealing with that stuff."

Humble, Dickey recognized that he didn't have all the answers. His therapist Stephen James gave Dickey exercises to maintain self-confidence. And Dickey would check in with Charlie Hough or ask Tim Wakefield if he would be willing to watch Dickey's last outing and see if he could pick up things that Dickey was doing that needed to be corrected.

An English major, Dickey was an avid reader in 2012 as he was during all seasons. Books provided a diversion and an outlet. Every season, he reread *The Power of One*, a coming-of-age story by Bryce Courtenay. During his Cy Young season, he enjoyed the novels *The Brothers K* by David James Duncan and *Life of Pi* by Yann Martel as well as revisiting classics by Hemingway and Fitzgerald.

"I absolutely love Hemingway, so *For Whom the Bell Tolls* is a favorite of mine," he says. "And short stories."

Dickey ended the year with a 20–6 record. His 2.73 ERA was the second lowest in the National League. He led the league in strikeouts (230), starts (33), complete games (five), shutouts (three), and innings pitched (233 2/3). Looking back, he says it was a fun season.

"Rarely do you get a chance in life, I think, to be that good at something and know that you're good at something," Dickey says. "There were moments when I felt like I could not be beaten. Not in an egomaniacal way. Just in a way where it's almost like you are doing what you were born to do, the way you were born to do it. Where you have a gift that you've been given, and you exercise that gift to the fullest. You feel a lot of satisfaction. Satisfied. That's the word. At the end of the season, I felt very satisfied because I felt like I had gotten the most out of myself."

He won the Cy Young Award by receiving 27 of 32 first-place votes. He learned he won the award while a live broadcast showed candidates Clayton Kershaw, Gio Gonzalez, and Dickey react to the envelope being opened and the winner announced. When Dickey's name was called, he was happy, but he remembers thinking: "This will not define me." R. A. Dickey, Cy Young Award winner.

"I want to be remembered as a good father, good husband. A God-fearing, kindhearted, generous, hardworking citizen," he says. "Those are attributes that people should value. I think a Cy Young is awesome. I just didn't want it to be the thing that was the most important thing about me."

The first knuckleball pitcher to win the award, Dickey was excited to share it with fellow knuckleballers Niekro, Wakefield, and Hough, who helped him discover and refine the pitch. And, as a 37-year-old with 17 seasons of professional baseball under his belt, Dickey felt a lot of gratitude. It was a long road to the Cy Young Award, and he had a lot of people to thank.

"I called people who I didn't talk to in probably five years just to thank them," Dickey says. "And I don't say that as a humblebrag. I'm saying that because I just felt this overwhelming sense of gratitude. That either someone had given me a chance to keep going, or Buck Showalter and Orel Hershiser were the two people that pointed me in that direction to be a knuckleballer in the first place. But there were no real fruits from it until six years later. So, they started me on a course that would change my life, and you don't get an opportunity to circle back around with those people very often and say, hey, man, thank you so much. I have a tangible thing to say look what you helped do. So, that was fun."

Lauded as the National League's best pitcher, Dickey was then traded to the Toronto Blue Jays along with Mike Nickeas and Josh Thole for John Buck, Travis d'Arnaud, Noah Syndergaard, and Wuilm-er Becerra.

"I understood it," he says. "[The Mets] wanted to capitalize on the year I had. They were going nowhere, and they knew it. And they were trying to figure out a way to grab the most out of what I had done."

And he was off to the Great White North, ready to begin a new climb and a new challenge. With no spin and a whisper at release.

# 10

# PITCHING AGGRESSIVELY: COREY KLUBER

## 2014 AND 2017 AMERICAN LEAGUE CY YOUNG AWARD

*When I spoke with Corey Kluber in December 2020, he had spent his morning working out at Cressey Sports Performance in Hudson, Massachusetts, in preparation to throw a bullpen for teams looking to add another starter. A free agent, Kluber was returning from his second injury in as many seasons. A broken forearm limited him to seven starts in 2019. He returned to pitch for the Texas Rangers during the pandemic-shortened 2020 season and threw exactly one inning before a shoulder injury shut him down for rest of the season. "With my shoulder, being that it was in the middle of the pandemic, I came back up here to Massachusetts to rehab it and be one less body for the team to keep track of, test, risk infecting others or getting infected, things like that," Kluber said. Although recovering from an injury can be challenging in many ways—a healing process that requires time and patience, a rehabilitation plan that tediously strengthens the repaired area, all while the athlete wants to rejoin his teammates and compete—Kluber was taking the long view. "I think it's just one of those things where you've got to get to the point where you have faith in what the doctor's telling you. You have faith in what the training staff's telling you. And you follow their guidelines, their directions. And if it's something as little as doing shoulder exercises and that's all you can do that day, just try to do those shoulder exercises as best as you possibly can, knowing that it's going to pay dividends in the long run even though it might be monotonous. It might feel like you're not really doing anything. I always just believe that, no matter what it is that I'm doing, I want to do the best that I can instead of just going through the motions on it."* [1]

Going into 2014, Corey Kluber had a positive outlook about the season ahead. The prior April, the Cleveland Indians called him up to fill in for injured Brett Myers. This was Kluber's third stint in the big leagues after spending parts of seven seasons in the minors. With this opportunity, Kluber clicked. He started 24 games, won 11 of them, and maintained a 3.85 ERA. [2] He ended the season by not losing a decision in his final 12 starts. Pleased with his progress, he was in the majors to stay.

"It probably gave me maybe a greater sense of confidence or self-belief that I did belong at that level, that I was able to pitch at that level and have some success," Kluber says. "I wouldn't say that I was ultra-consistent, so to speak. I think I showed flashes of consistency. There were still times when things maybe weren't as consistent as I would like, but it gave me confidence to know that I was able to go out there and pitch well and help the team. Whereas, the year before, in 2012 when I was up there for an extended amount of time, I was still trying to figure out my way and not step on anybody's toes, all that kind of stuff that happens a lot of times with young guys. I think that hampers your ability to go out there and perform when you're on the field until you get that level of comfort."

After 2013, Kluber spent his offseason as he had prior offseasons—working to build his body back up, then moving to throwing, before progressing to fine-tuning his pitches so he would be ready for spring training and the 162-game season ahead that would call on him to make at least 30 starts. He didn't set lofty goals of winning X games or ringing up Y strikeouts. Instead, he concentrated on doing the things within his control well. How he prepared in between starts. How he challenged hitters.

"I know there's different trains of thoughts," Kluber says. "Some people say if you're your best individually, it helps the team. Others say if you're the best you can be for the team, it helps you individually. I think I fall more in line with that one. I just tried to go out there and help the team win games and compete—that's what has always made me to be my best."

The season started slowly. By the end of April, he was 2–3 with a 4.14 ERA. But Kluber remained committed to his preparation. Pitching coach Mickey Callaway praised Kluber for being locked in during his bullpens throughout the season. Not only were the sessions helpful to ensure aligned mechanics and that Kluber was producing a consistent, repeatable delivery, something he says is essential to producing good pitches, but the sessions were crucial for executing mentally during games.

"The more realistic, the more gamelike I can make the bullpen, the more natural it's going to feel to me on the mound with that level of focus and intensity," he says. "Going through the motions, it just doesn't really work for me. I don't do a good job of executing pitches if I'm not going at a pretty intense effort level. It just turns into a waste of time. So, that's just always been what I've had to do to get the most out of it."

As April ended, Kluber threw his first career complete game, beating Kansas City 5–1 at home and delivering a performance that Ohio newspapers touted as the best by a Cleveland pitcher since Len Barker threw a perfect game in 1981. Indeed, Kluber didn't allow a walk or an earned run. He struck out 11, then a career-high mark. In his next start, he allowed only one run and three hits while striking out 13. During a stretch from the third to the fifth innings, Kluber struck out seven consecutive hitters, a performance so dominant that it prompted Cleveland manager Terry Francona to say, "That's about as good as you can pitch."[3] On the road in Kansas City in July, Kluber had a perfect game going into the seventh inning as he retired the first 19 batters. In his next start, he threw his first career shutout, a 2–0 win over Seattle, beating 2010 American League Cy Young Award winner Felix Hernandez. Needing only 85 pitches for his complete game, Kluber faced 28 hitters, one over the minimum, and threw only 16 pitches that were balls. In September, he had back-to-back games with 14 strikeouts.

While Kluber points to his commitment to practice and preparation as one of his keys to success, other factors contributed as well. One was using the two-seam fastball. Generally, the four-seam fastball is a pitcher's fastest and straightest pitch, and, to hitters, the ball appears to rise as it approaches the plate. The pitch gets its name from what the batter sees when the pitcher releases the ball: four seams with each rotation as the ball spins. Roger Clemens relied heavily on his four-seamer as he won more Cy Young Awards than anyone in baseball history. In contrast, with the two-seam fastball, the pitcher grips the ball by placing his two fingers directly on top of the ball where the seams are closest together. Typically, two-seamers are a touch slower compared to the four-seam fastball, and they spin less. They have more movement, though, moving in the same direction as the arm throwing the ball (e.g., a right-handed pitcher like Kluber gets rightward movement on a two-seamer), making the ball harder to hit. Greg Maddux mastered the two-seam fastball (as did Jim Lonborg during the offseason prior to his 1967 campaign), and, with Kluber's mechanics, arm angle, and release point, the two-seamer was a great pitch for him to throw. Plus, its grip was more comfortable for him.

"That's probably what helped my career more than anything is finding a fastball I can locate where I want to," he says. "I can feel confident throwing it and not be defensive with it. Early on in the minors, I didn't command my four-seam fastball very well and therefore didn't have a whole lot of confidence in it. Finding a fastball that I could locate, it opened everything else up for me. It kind of freed me up to throw that pitch aggressively, and then the more I could throw that pitch for strikes, throw it where I wanted to, it allowed me to throw my off-speed stuff more in certain situations."

Kluber had also read *The Mental ABCs of Pitching* by H. A. Dorfman, a longtime mental training consultant with the Oakland A's, Florida Marlins, and Tampa Bay Rays. The book, described as "a handbook for performance enhancement," addresses concepts like aggressiveness, body language, concentration, and confidence. Kluber found the instructions and tips for how to focus and act on the mound invaluable.

"It broke things down into a very simplistic way," he says. "The way it registered with me is going out there and simplifying things on the mound and have an aggressive mind-set and stuff like that. It's all stuff that sounds elementary, but you kind of have to train yourself to do those things in the heat of the moment and not get wrapped up in all the things that are easy to get wrapped up in."

Open to new ideas, be it trying a two-seam fastball or reading a book to learn more about pitching, Kluber believes in doing whatever he can to improve. "I've always tried to pick things up along the way from different people, whether it be guys that I played with, whether it be coaches. Just that constant mentality of trying to learn things. Greg Maddux is a good example. He talks about how he learned stuff when he was 40 years old, or he learned stuff now that he wished he knew when he was playing."

One resource for Kluber in both seasons he won the Cy Young Award was catcher Yan Gomes. Gomes, who signed a six-year, $23 million contract with the Indians at the beginning of 2014, was valued for his offensive production as well as for the counsel he provided pitchers to make them feel more comfortable and be more effective. At this point in Kluber's career, he was still in an early learning stage of facing big-league hitters and trying to figure out when and how to adjust to them after they adjusted to him. Kluber relied on Gomes for guidance.

"He helped me grow up and learn a lot as a pitcher and not just going out there and throwing whatever pitch it is, but setting up guys for later on in that at-bat, setting guys up for later on in the game, setting up guys for the next time you face them, however far down the road."

Kluber admires Gomes's game planning and how he strove to put his pitcher in a position to succeed. As a result, when Gomes signed for a pitch, Kluber went along with the suggestion. A consistent presence, Gomes caught 32 of Kluber's 34 starts in 2014 and 26 of 29 in 2017.

"We worked well together," Kluber says. "We communicated well with each other. We were friends, first and foremost, before pitcher-catcher, and I think that I was able to see how much he cared about leading a pitching staff, how much time and preparation he put into game plans. The kind of behind-the-scenes stuff, I think that frees you up to have full trust in him. When he's putting fingers down, you know it's not just a guess on his part, but there's actually a very profound reason and ideas behind what he's doing."

Looking back on this season when he emerged as an elite pitcher, the moments that stand out to Kluber are in September when his team, around .500, was competing against long odds for a wild-card berth.

"In 2013, we made the postseason," he says. "The end of that season, being in the middle of a playoff push, that extra intensity, how much fun those games are—it's, as much as you want to try to treat every game the same, they are different when you get to that level, when it gives you that excitement and energy with it. In 2014, we didn't make the playoffs, but going into the last week of the season, we still weren't eliminated. There was a mathematical chance, and we were feeding off that feeling of hey, teams have done it before. You go out there and win every game. Crazier things have happened. Trying to feed off that energy at the end of the season, trying to do something that nobody thinks you can do. I always like those moments."

The Indians finished the season with an 85–77 mark, third in the American League Central. Kluber ended the season with an 18–9 record and a 2.44 ERA. He led the AL in wins and games started (34). He struck out 269, second most in the league. And he won the Cy Young Award, beating out Felix Hernandez 169 points to 159 and collecting more first-place ballots (17) than anyone else.

Kluber credits his success to pitching aggressively. He threw strikes and got ahead in the count. He rarely walked anyone (in 2014, he had 51 walks in 235 2/3 innings).

"Obviously, making quality pitches is important, but, more than anything, pounding the strike zone, putting the hitter on the defensive. Dictating at-bats: I think that's the key to pitching or hitting," he says. "I think that, more often than not, the guy who controls the at-bat, the guy who's the aggressor, as long as they can execute in that position, whether they be pitching or hitting, I think those are the guys that ultimately wind up having success more consistently."

In addition to challenging hitters with good pitches to hit, Kluber kept hitters guessing.

"I'm not going to rear back and blow a fastball by guys," he says. "Whether you want to call it movement, deception, whatever it is, I think there's a level of that that I have to rely on. So, the longer I can keep my pitches looking the same to a hitter, it gives them that much less time to decide what it is. There's plenty of guys with a ton of movement on the ball. I think that the guys who maybe give hitters a little bit more of a fit are the ones who it's moving late. They can't decipher what it is until it's almost too late for them to pull the trigger or make a decision to sit on something. It's kind of that old phrase of keeping hitters off-balance is kind of the way I do it. And keep hitters off-balance with movement and speed, front to back, changing speeds."

Although Kluber was the American League's best pitcher, his season wasn't without blemishes. His first start was a loss where he didn't pitch past the fourth inning. Kluber, though, struck a balance to learn from a loss and move on and not dwell on failure.

"It's disappointing, but I think that ultimately, if you know that you prepared the best you can, you did everything you can to put yourself in the best position possible to go out there and succeed, it's not always going to happen that way," he says. "There's going to be times when the hitters get the best of you or days when you just don't have it, but, if you know that you did everything within your power to put yourself in the best spot you can, I think you can live with that, and you're able to move on pretty quickly and flush it. I think if you have the what-ifs—what if I had done more of this? Spent more time on this? That's probably when it eats away at you a little more and things kind of start to snowball. For me, the easiest way to handle failure is just prepare myself the best I can, and then I can live with the results, whether they're good or bad."

Kluber continued pitching at a high level in 2015 and '16. In 2015, Kluber struck out 18 St. Louis Cardinals in his first win of the season on May 13. He threw a one-hitter against the Twins on August 14. During the regular season in 2016, he again won 18 games and led the American League in shutouts (two). The Indians won their division and charged through the playoffs to clinch the American League pennant and reach the World Series to face the Chicago Cubs. During the post-season, Kluber made six starts, including wins in Games One and Four in the World Series. The added experience and high level of success meant Kluber was a different pitcher going into 2017 than he was when he began the 2014 season, pleased with his prior performance during his first full big-league season and wanting to build on that success. At this point, Kluber was one of the game's elite.

"[By] 2017, I feel like I had a better grasp on [setting up pitches]," he says.

He began the season by making six starts. Then he missed nearly the entire month of May because of a lower back strain.

"I think just the workload of the playoffs the year before, my body never had a chance to fully recover going into that year," he says. "That break was probably a blessing in disguise, in May. I think it allowed me to feel really good when I came back; 2017 was more of a, I don't know if culmination is the right word, but all of the different pieces coming together. Physical, mental to where it felt like I was in a really good spot after I missed time in all those areas and just kind of hit the ground running when I came back and took off from there."

Kluber returned from the injured list and faced Oakland at home on June 1.

"The moment for me that probably stands out most from 2017 is the first game back after I was on the DL," he says. "I probably didn't realize just how much the playoff run in 2016 took out of me, and I was pitching the first part of '17 pretty beat up. The time off allowed me to really get things right, and my first outing back I think I went something like six innings, ten Ks. But, more importantly, I felt like I was able to move the way I wanted to on the mound and execute pitches the way I expect of myself. After that, it was kind of like, 'alright, here we go.'"4

The excellent work against Oakland, facing 20 batters and allowing only two hits and one walk and no runs, continued as Kluber compiled a string of impressive starts: shutting out Baltimore while giving up only three hits. Striking out 14 against Toronto. Pitching consecutive complete games, a 5–1 win against the Yankees followed by a 4–1 win over Colorado. From June 1 through August 13, Kluber pitched 14 consecutive games with at least eight strikeouts, one game shy of tying Randy Johnson's record. As Kluber rolled, so did his teammates. From August 24, Cleveland caught fire and won 22 consecutive games, the longest winning streak since the 2002 Oakland A's won 20 games in a row. On the mound as the Indians sought their 20th straight win? Kluber, who delivered a complete-game shutout over the Tigers, 2–0.

"The most memorable part of the winning streak was probably the last win, Jay Bruce's walk-off," Kluber says, referring to the September 14 game at home against Kansas City that went into extra innings. In the bottom of the 10th with no outs and runners at second and first, Bruce hit a line drive to right field to seal the Indians' 22nd consecutive victory. "Once we got to probably eighteen or so wins, people *really* started coming out to the ballpark, and it felt like a playoff atmosphere. That specific game was pretty intense. The Royals were a division rival; I'm sure they really wanted to be the ones to end our winning streak; and we wanted to keep it going. All those things and then a walkoff win on top of it makes that game stand out most to me."5

Amid Cleveland's late-season surge, Kluber likewise compiled an individual streak. He threw 32 innings in September without giving up an earned run. Kluber says he wasn't doing anything special or different during the streak.

"I don't remember much about that scoreless streak," he says. "And, honestly, that's probably why it happened, because I wasn't focusing on it. It was no different than any other time out for me, just try to go out and pitch the best with what I have that day and give the team a chance to win."[6]

As the season wound down, Cleveland clinched the American League Central Division. Although hot from their win streak, the Indians fell short in the first round of the playoffs, losing the Division Series to the Yankees two games to three. Nonetheless, voters still noted Kluber's outstanding performance as the best on an American League mound in 2017. Earning 28 of a total 30 first-place votes, Kluber won his second Cy Young Award with his 18–4 record and 2.25 ERA, lowest in the American League. Kluber was honored to win the award, but he acknowledges that the individual recognition represents the work and contributions of many.

"Cy Young awards don't happen without tons of other people, mostly behind the scenes," Kluber says. "Obviously, Yan played a key role, and I think we'll always have those years to look back on as something we accomplished together, regardless of whose name is on an award. But, also coaches, trainers, strength coaches, scouts, front office, video, clubhouse guys—they all play a role in anyone's success and rarely get the credit they deserve for it."[7]

# CONCLUSION

*You can throw the ball hardest. You can throw it softest. As long as you know what you're doing, you can win. You can beat anybody.—*
Ron Guidry[1]

**O**bserving celebrated Cy Young Award–winning seasons by pitchers with different strengths and backgrounds illustrates that there is more than one way to succeed. Indeed, the book begins with Jim Lonborg in 1967 as a 25-year-old in his third big-league season. Lonborg threw hard and inside. He won 22 games and led the league in wins, games started, strikeouts, and batters hit by pitches.[2] Toward the end of the book, R. A. Dickey, a 37-year-old in his 17th season of professional baseball, also won the Cy Young Award. Relying on an 80-mph knuckleball, he too led the league in wins, games started, and strikeouts. Two very different approaches by pitchers at different stages of their careers, yet both succeeded at the highest level and were recognized as the best in their field. They share commonalities beyond winning the Cy Young Award. Cerebral and college educated (Lonborg at Stanford, Dickey at the University of Tennessee), both studied pitching and understood how to make the ball move. Both found a diversion to prevent baseball from becoming all-consuming (Lonborg liked to watch a matinee movie on days he pitched; Dickey read novels). Lonborg and Dickey enjoyed the partner they worked with behind the plate. That said, their seasons had differences. Lonborg was a part of the pennant-winning Red Sox. He pitched some of his best games in the postseason against the St. Louis Cardinals. In contrast, Dickey's Mets finished in fourth place in the National League East. Dickey had a manager he could confide in with Terry Collins; in contrast, gruff Dick Williams was not someone Lonborg chatted with. In fact, Lonborg strove to prove that he was better than Williams thought he was.

Still, similarities exist. And by looking at these pitchers' successful seasons and distilling the common threads, we may discover something that worked for one or more of them that is helpful to a young pitcher in high school, college, or the minor leagues. Or, maybe that pitcher takes that idea and adjusts it slightly so it works well for him. Zooming out further, the principles that helped shape these athletes into better pitchers can transcend the baseball diamond and apply in the classroom or workplace as effective tools to use generally.

## ADAPTING

> There would be funny stories like you warm up in the bullpen, and your stuff would just be lights out, and the catcher would look at you and say, "There's no fucking way anybody's going to hit you today." And you felt it too because you would see the way the ball was jumping. And you would go out to the mound, and you wouldn't get through the first inning because your head is not as focused. . . . Then there would be days when the catcher would say, "You know, you don't have shit. Good luck." And then you would go out there and throw a shutout. Because mentally, now you know you just have to concentrate so hard to make good pitches. And then, all of a sudden, things just start to roll together, and before you know it, then the game's over, and you've got a shutout and you've given up five hits just because your head and your body are together.—Jim Lonborg[3]

Although they may have been the best pitcher on their team or even in the major leagues, these pitchers were open to trying new ideas. In some cases, it was to hang on and stay in the big leagues. For others, it was listening to suggestions that led to improvements, and, in some instances, those improvements propelled great to exceptional. Sometimes, it meant making on-the-fly tweaks and buckling down to execute these adjustments. Though the circumstances varied, the pitchers had the humility to recognize that they didn't have all the answers, and they had the curiosity and willingness to consider different ways for improving their craft.

Mike McCormick was one of the best left-handed pitchers in the late 1950s and early 1960s. But a shoulder injury compromised his ability to pitch, much less to pitch at a dominant level. He could have quit playing and moved to the next phase of his life. He could have pressed on, trying to recapture what worked well when he was 20 or 21 and his shoulder was functioning optimally and he was named to consecutive All-Star teams. But that path wasn't a realistic one. He had to find a different way to be successful. And he listened to his pitching coach George Susce, who encouraged him to develop the screwball as an off-speed pitch. Through a grind of repetition, of hours playing catch on the outfield grass with Susce repeating, "Turn it over. Turn it over," reminding McCormick to supinate his wrist, he found a new way to get batters out effectively. He served as a jack-of-all-trades for the Washington Senators in 1965, starting 21 games and making 23 relief appearances. The Giants picked him up in December 1966 to be an innings eater, and the screwball he had been working on for the past few seasons baffled National League hitters. He led the league with 22 wins.

R. A. Dickey offers a similar illustration. After shuttling back and forth from the minors to the majors, he accepted the advice of Buck Showalter and Orel Hershiser and shifted from conventional fastball, curveball, and changeup pitching to becoming a knuckleballer. Like McCormick devoting hours to practicing a new release for a new pitch, Dickey poured himself into working with mentors, learning, and practicing.

"It's different," he says. "Your whole life you're taught to throw this certain way—you're having to unlearn that. And relearn a whole different mechanic. It's like someone coming to you as a [right-hander] and saying, 'Okay, I want you to learn to write left-handed.' Go ahead and do that. It's hard. Like you've got to deconstruct because the mechanics are so different, the mind-set's so different, the wrist position's different, the stride length's different, the leverage points are different. Everything's different except you're throwing it overhand, just like you would conventionally."[4]

Dickey worked through this unfamiliarity, a disconnect with nearly everything he had known and honed before. And it paid off. Not only did he land in the majors to stay, but it was also with Dickey serving as a reliable anchor in the starting rotation, good for 30 starts and 200 innings season after season.

Although he didn't learn a new pitch, Dennis Eckersley changed roles drastically midstream in his career. He went from starting 30 to 35 games a season to relief pitching, ultimately as a specialist to get the final three outs of the game. The new role meant Eckersley had to adjust. The routine he used during his prior 12 seasons as a starter had to be modified as he now needed to be ready to play every day as opposed to pitching every fifth day. And he needed a new mind-set for dealing with pressure, all eyes on him, the win entrusted to him to preserve, a different type of pressure from starting pitching, and, frankly, a stress that some don't have the makeup to handle. Having a fresh start in life after attending a rehabilitation clinic for alcohol abuse, Eckersley was open to the new role.

"I sort of ran out of gas," he says. "So I went to the bullpen, and my fastball came back. Because I didn't need it for six or seven innings. I used it for one."[5]

He thought his time in the bullpen would be short term and that he would return to the starting rotation as the season progressed, but he settled into a new role and became one of the game's all-time great closers.

These are extreme examples of adapting, but most of these pitchers could not rely solely on their talent as is and stick with what worked well in the past and ensure success in the major leagues, much less be the best pitcher in the American or National League in a given year. They accepted that adjustments were needed to take that talent to the next level. In some instances, they listened to a pitching coach's suggestion about how to pitch. Red Sox pitching coach Sal Maglie preached the importance of throwing inside to hitters, that it kept them uncomfortable and took the outside part of the strike zone away from them. Jim Lonborg embraced the concept wholeheartedly during his Cy Young season, even applying it to the first pitch he threw in the World Series to communicate to Lou Brock that he shouldn't get too comfortable in the box because the plate was Lonborg's, not the hitter's.

Sometimes, finding another way to be effective involved trying a new pitch. Teammate Sparky Lyle showed Ron Guidry how to refine his slider and provided Guidry another tool to use during the rare opportunities he was allowed to pitch when he first joined the Yankees and was unproven in manager Billy Martin's eyes. When thrown into some emergency starts, Guidry had that resource to tap into and achieve success. Using it in 1977, Guidry won 16 games. The next year, his win total jumped to 25. In San Diego, Randy Jones displayed similar success after learning the sinker from Padres pitching instructor Warren Hacker. After a few weeks of experimenting with the pitch, Jones loved how much the ball dropped. Once he implemented it into his repertoire, he used it to induce countless groundballs and made it a core of his pitching. Corey Kluber explored using his two-seam fastball instead of his four-seamer. He discovered better control, more confidence, and a greater ability to mix off-speed pitches in to keep hitters off-balance.

Pitchers showed an appreciation for continued learning off the field as well. Throughout his career, LaMarr Hoyt studied pitching. From conversations with minor-league teammate Michael Rusk, Hoyt began to view pitching in terms of aerodynamic movements. With fellow White Sox starter Richard Dotson, Hoyt stayed up late into the night, discussing how they faced batters. When Tom Seaver joined the White Sox, Hoyt saw how Seaver used the rubber as a projectile to push from, confirming his theory of how the mound should be used. Hoyt *loved* the art of pitching, analyzing it down to the detail of knowing if his middle finger was damp with sweat, the ball would move one way and if his index finger was damp, it would move another. And Hoyt wasn't afraid to experiment with these ideas and see how they worked.

Corey Kluber, the only active pitcher profiled, vouches for being open to new ideas. "Having that mind-set of trying to always learn, there's always an opportunity to gain things from different people, no matter what their role is or anything like that."[6]

Learning involves vulnerability. Trying a new pitch, a new role, a new approach to facing a batter, the pitcher risks failing. He may embarrass himself as the hitter greets the experiment by teeing off for a dinger. Amid the newness, the pitcher may have moments of feeling out of sync and unnatural. He may want to reject the suggestion and return to the known and the comfortable that have carried him to this already advanced point. Nonetheless, these pitchers accepted trying alternatives. They were willing to explore whether a new factor or approach made them better. Importantly, a fear of failure or of feeling uncomfortable as they tried something new didn't stop them. They pushed through the awkward stage. And then they flourished.

## PREPARING

*I used to run every day. You would think I was pitching nine innings, you know? I would run 20 miles a week. I was into it. So, I represented how you went about doing it. Sort of that consistency.*—Dennis Eckersley

Not one of these pitchers relied on talent alone to carry them to success. All of them prepared for the grind of standing on the mound, April to October, and launching a baseball repetitively at a high speed. Jack McDowell spent his offseason firing a baseball against a church's brick wall and fielding 200 groundballs. He also loved to get on the slide board and concentrate on maintaining that explosive first-step movement. Ron Guidry sprinted to catch fly balls during batting practice. LaMarr Hoyt rode a bicycle on the streets of Columbia, South Carolina, during the offseason and hopped on a stationary bicycle throughout the season to maintain his cardiovascular system. During his offseason, Randy Jones enjoyed running pass patterns and catching a football for his cardio workout. Dennis Eckersley was a distance runner, logging four miles daily. Barry Zito embraced stretching, yoga, and long toss. Jim Lonborg skied to develop and maintain a strong core. R. A. Dickey trained to and then climbed the highest mountain in Africa. Each pitcher found a way to exercise and maintain his body for the 162-game schedule, and it was something that worked well for him. Again, the varied approaches illustrate that there is more than one way to accomplish success with no standard recipe to follow of run X number of poles to ensure pitching achievements. Pitching is strenuous work, though, and the pitchers all prioritized conditioning to position themselves to be able to perform the task of throwing baseballs over and over throughout the course of six months.

Not only did these pitchers prepare their bodies to physically perform, but they also prepared mentally to pitch. Randy Jones watched hitters and noted their likes and dislikes and "made a living" pitching to their weaknesses. LaMarr Hoyt had a similar eye of observing the pitches that hitters wanted and which ones they preferred avoiding and, in turn, feeding them what they didn't want. Though Hoyt could size up a batter by the way he was standing in the box and deduce what pitches the hitter was looking for, he studied hitters' tendencies and used this information to inform where he placed the ball. During bullpens, R. A. Dickey envisioned the upcoming lineup he was going to face, and he practiced for those situations down to what and where he would throw for a first pitch to a specific hitter, followed by the next pitches in the sequence. Moreover, he prioritized this work. "I would never miss [a bullpen]. I was just vehement about not missing," he says. "I would start; I would take one day off after my start, and then I would throw a pen. Every single time." Corey Kluber echoes Dickey, making his bullpen sessions as close to gamelike conditions as possible. When Randy Jones practiced in the bullpen, he concentrated on hitting exact spots because, during a game, he wanted the certainty of knowing he could hit a precise target for a strike.

Pitchers took the work they did before the game—both physical and mental—seriously. Understanding their opponent and knowing how to attack them was key. Hollywood may present idyllic moments of a young Roy Hobbs raring back and blasting the ball past the Whammer in *The Natural*, and indeed, some pitchers can rely on a God-given ability to smoke a ball with tricky movement past hitters. But these pitchers typically used a blended approach, of building their arm and their body to be in a position to perform and, while doing so, made informed decisions about the pitches they were throwing, tailored to that batter, to improve the chances of getting an out instead of someone getting on base.

## HAVING A NETWORK

*Going into that season, I kind of knew where we stood. I had climbed that ladder and was, okay, this is how you do this. I pretty much knew that was going to be what I did, which was to win upper-teens games, throw eight innings a start, finish as many games as they let me, and try to drag everybody else into the team philosophy that we're going to win this thing and go to the playoffs.*—Jack McDowell[7]

Pitching can be an isolated experience—one man, alone, on the mound, holding a ball in his hand, looking at his catcher, and executing a game plan to prevent the batter from making hard contact. Despite the solitary nature, these men connected with others as a source of support. And finding that larger connection made them stronger pitchers.

In some cases, the pitchers were part of a close-knit team. For Jim Lonborg, the '67 Red Sox enjoyed each other on and off the field. Lonborg praised his defense for making plays and the offense for timely and consistent production. After games, teammates regularly went out to dinner together. They laughed and created a buoyant camaraderie for all, including Lonborg, a self-described quiet and introspective man who enjoyed spending free time reading or visiting a museum or a historical site. Jack McDowell's 1993 Chicago White Sox likewise had excellent offense, defense, and team chemistry. Like the '67 Red Sox, the '93 White Sox reached the postseason. Both prioritized the collective and the team achieving its goals over an individual and his stat line. McDowell felt pangs whenever the general manager made trades or roster changes because those moves involved *his guys*. Together since spring training, they chased a goal, trying to get past the powerhouse Oakland dynasty, and it wounded McDowell when a piece of the team left. McDowell and third baseman Robin Ventura set the tone that they would do whatever it took to win and leave every bit of talent, effort, and determination on the field. The team fed off that energy and maintained a *team* environment, a strong commitment that resulted in better play behind McDowell when he was pitching. The 2002 Oakland A's also had great team chemistry as they won a then–American League record 20 consecutive games and the American League Western Division. Their blend of veteran and young players was a welcome combination for Barry Zito. With fellow starter Tim Hudson, he could cut up and relax in between starts. He could watch Mark Mulder pitch and be in absolute awe of his stuff. Teammates Scott Hatteberg and David Justice served as father figures, offering advice and support to the 24-year-old Zito, playing in his third major-league season. And just as Lonborg appreciated the great catches and throws by Jose Tartabull and Carl Yastrzemski, Zito was grateful for Miguel Tejada and his dependability at shortstop in scooping up grounders and starting double plays and for Terrence Long covering center field and chasing down fly balls.

Ron Guidry had multiple networks. When Guidry reached the big leagues, relief pitchers Sparky Lyle and Dick Tidrow took him under their wings and welcomed him and made him feel comfortable. They gave him a nickname. They joked with him and lit his shoelaces on fire. They showed him a new pitch, and they made the new major leaguer better. Likewise, Guidry leaned on his coaching staff for guidance. Lucky to have Yogi Berra and Elston Howard with a combined 33 years of big-league catching experience serving on the coaching staff, Guidry regularly checked in with his elders for advice on what he could be doing better. And like Lonborg, McDowell, and Zito, Guidry was part of a team that clicked. Today, when he sees former teammates Ed Figueroa, Rich Gossage, and Graig Nettles, the bonds they developed more than 40 years ago when they won the World Series in 1978 remain. Teammates pick right up where they left off, as if it were just yesterday when they shared the clubhouse in Yankee Stadium.

As Jim Lonborg left Stanford, his coach encouraged him to find a mentor in the professional ranks. Specifically, he advised Lonborg to look for the hardest-working pitcher on the team.

"Eventually befriend that person and realize that what he can teach you will make you a better ballplayer."

Lonborg listened. And watched. And saw that Bill Monbouquette "ran more than any human being I had ever seen in my life."

So Lonborg approached Monbouquette and asked, "Do you mind if I run with you?"

"Sure."

Which led to a kind of partnership, two talented runners, pushing each other, making the other better. And friends off the field who could share a pitcher of beer and some laughs and some stories—and build a connection.

Like Guidry, Lonborg found multiple mentors. As a rookie, he shared a locker with Earl Wilson, a veteran with five years of experience.

"Earl taught me about how to conduct yourself," Lonborg says. "He was a big, tall, handsome black guy that had a swagger about him, and he was always talking about creating a presence on the mound. One of intimidation and self-confidence. And you had to feel that way on and off the field. You had a responsibility to be something more than just an athlete. You had to be a citizen. You had to do things for the team and always conduct yourself in a gentlemanly way."

R. A. Dickey belonged to the knuckleball fraternity. From Phil Niekro, Charlie Hough, and Tim Wakefield, Dickey sought advice and instruction. Although Hough told Dickey to be prepared to be his best coach, Dickey also had this network to rely on for tutelage. "Every time that [Tim Wakefield] would come in town, I'd be like a sponge," Dickey says. "I'd just be like a suction fish all over him, you know, if he'd let me. And he did. He was—all those guys are so accommodating. I mean, what other sport are you going to get to go and watch him throw his bullpens? We're trying to beat this other team, and he's teaching me how to do it well. The fraternity is so empathetic. Because we all know how hard it is to get the thing right, you know?"

It's crucial to have a network to tap into. A pitcher is not going to find all the answers within. If the pitcher has someone else to look to for help, be it guidance, support, and/or laughter, it's essential. It makes the pitcher better. And there is no need to reinvent the wheel. If someone has already gone through what the pitcher is experiencing and can offer help or suggestions to make the other pitcher's path a little easier to travel, why not take advantage of the insight and accept those lessons learned? With that network to rely on for support, the pitcher is that much stronger than if he goes it alone, sticking with one mind-set, one skill set, one set of experiences—his own. True, the individual or singular path may produce exceptional success. In theory, a pitcher could rely entirely on himself and retire batter after batter with strikeouts or easy comebackers to the mound, and the pitcher could jog toward the first baseline to get all 27 outs in the game. But the pitcher is only *one* part of the team. And I, me, and my are only so effective. "You've got your team behind you, you won't understand how much better it is," Jack McDowell says. The pitcher is stronger and the team is stronger when the pitcher relies on the team, not himself. As Ron Guidry says, he knew he could throw an inside slider to a right-handed hitter and that Graig Nettles would scoop it up at third. Chris Chambliss would handle anything on the opposite side of the diamond at first, and speedy Mickey Rivers would track anything down in center field. Counting on the team behind him, "you could go out to pitch an inning and throw three pitches and get out," Guidry says.

## TRUSTING YOUR PARTNER

*Let's say there was a 1–2 count, and I'm throwing my best knuckle-ball ever. So, it would be really uncharacteristic for me to get a fastball 1–2. So there would be times when [Josh Thole, the catcher] would give me fastball, and I'd go no. And he would give it to me again, and then I would realize he sees something. Whether the hitter is moving up in the batter's box or he knew that his approach was going to be to wait back and try to hit the knuckleball to right field, and I could throw it by him inside. So, we had this thing where, if he would give [the sign] to me twice, I didn't question it ever.—R. A. Dickey*

For each pitch, the pitcher looks to the catcher, who performs multiple duties. The catcher should present a good target. He should understand the pitcher's strengths and weaknesses as well as the batter's while also factoring in the home plate umpire's strike zone and make informed suggestions for pitch selection. He should work in rhythm with the pitcher. If the pitcher likes a fast pace, the catcher needs to keep up accordingly. The catcher needs to be a resource for the pitcher, some-one who senses when it's time for a breather, when it's time for encour-agement, and when it's time for a kick in the ass to challenge the pitcher. The bottom line is the catcher should be the pitcher's partner whom the pitcher trusts so that when the catcher signs for a pitch, the pitcher doesn't second-guess or even think. He can be on autopilot and focus entirely on executing the pitch.

This type of partnership isn't instant. It takes time to develop. The season before he won the Cy Young Award, Ron Guidry worked pri-marily with Thurman Munson as Munson caught 25 of Guidry's 31 appearances. In 1978, it jumped to catching 29 of 33 games. For Randy Jones, he worked with his main catcher Fred Kendall in 82 games prior to 1976 when Jones won the Cy Young Award. Similarly, R. A. Dickey worked with Josh Thole over two seasons and developed a rapport with him before Dickey's Cy Young season. Barry Zito was comfortable part-nering with Ramon Hernandez in 2002 because the two already had a track record—Hernandez caught him 29 times in 2001. This familiarity creates conditions where batteries work in sync. The pitcher trusts the catcher's pitch selections, and the pitcher doesn't second-guess the catcher.

"Ramon was kind of like my guy," Zito says. "He caught me ever since I came up, so Ramon knew me inside out. I'll still look at game tapes from that '01–'02 run, and I'm not shaking almost ever. I mean, Ramon was putting down what I had thought in my head the second before."[8]

A quarter century earlier, Randy Jones and Fred Kendall were clicking similarly. They shared the same mind-set of Kendall knowing what pitch to call and Jones thinking, "Yes!" when he saw the sign for it. In addition, Kendall knew when it was time to adjust. Jones liked to work fast, sometimes too fast. With a simple gesture of placing his palms down, signaling Jones to tap on the brakes, Kendall communicated that it was time to slow down. Doing so kept Jones out of harm's way.

A catcher could defer entirely to the pitcher's inclinations, but, using Randy Jones and Fred Kendall as an example, that's not the way a partnership should work. Kendall *could* have let Jones keep working fast. After all, Jones was one of the best pitchers in the major leagues, with talk that he might be the first to win 30 games in a season since Denny McLain. Why not let the superstar in the spotlight do what he wants? Because no one, not even the superstar on the cover of *Sports Illustrated*, has all the answers. A good partner has the courage to step up and let his counterpart know he's getting ready to make a misstep. He offers to show him a more productive route. He sees something the pitcher is missing, and he shares this to get the pitcher back on track. "I was such a control pitcher," LaMarr Hoyt says. "Carlton Fisk, he'd have to stare at me sometimes and give me a sign where it was just a fist. It meant, 'Knock the guy down. You're around the plate too much.' So, just knock the guy down. Make him uncomfortable."[9]

## DEALING WITH FAILURE AND HAVING RESILIENCE

Dennis Eckersley pitched 24 seasons and appeared in more than 1,000 games in the major leagues. When asked what moments stand out from his playing career, he says, "The moment that stands out, obviously, it sounds corny, well, you have two. The '88 World Series with the Gibson thing."

"The Gibson thing." The often-replayed scene of Game One of the 1988 World Series. Eckersley came in to pitch the bottom of the ninth with the score A's 4, Dodgers 3, notch three outs, and preserve an A's win to stake them to an early lead in the Series. Eckersley retired the first two batters before walking Mike Davis. Then Kirk Gibson, battling a pulled hamstring, pinch-hit. In a 3–2 count, Gibson hit a line drive to deep right field that cleared the fence and ended the game for a Dodgers win. Gibson limped as he touched the bases, pumping his fist, and Eckersley walked off the mound, dejected.

The Dodgers went on to win the Series, four games to one. But Eckersley and the A's didn't go away. In 1989, they roared back. Eckersley earned 33 saves with a tiny 1.56 ERA. The A's won 99 games and the American League pennant, and they returned to the World Series to face the San Francisco Giants.

"Then, the next year [1989] was the Earthquake Series that almost didn't restart, right?" Eckersley says. "I got the last out. A play at first. The ball in my hand. That's thank you very much. After the year before, are you kidding me? To be able to come back the next year and win it? And, I'm from California, San Francisco Giants fan, and Candlestick Park, the whole thing. Can't forget that."

Baseball is a game of failure, mixed with the wins and triumphs, but undoubtedly, a pitcher will fail. He will lose games. In crucial situations, he may give up a hit and allow the go-ahead run to score. Maybe he threw the wrong pitch. Maybe he threw the right pitch and executed it perfectly. Maybe the defense was poorly positioned. Maybe the defense muffed the play. Maybe the umpire missed a call. Maybe the manager made a tactical mistake. Regardless, the breaks aren't always going to fall the pitcher's way. And the successful pitcher will find a way to put the disappointment or failure behind him. The pitcher can't let it carry over to the next game or even to the next at-bat. Learn from it at the appropriate time and move on.

Mike McCormick bounced back from an injury, a trade, and a demotion to the minor leagues to stick with his craft, learn a new way of performing it, and return to succeed with a different approach. Randy Jones led the National League in losses in 1974 with 22. He tired toward the end of games, and, as a result, his sinker quit sinking. Instead of tucking tail or discarding the pitch, Jones dedicated himself to his conditioning to improve his endurance and pitch longer in games with greater effectiveness. The following season, he posted the lowest earned-run average in the National League. The next season, he led the league in wins and won the Cy Young Award. After R. A. Dickey experienced a difficult outing, he journaled about the game or talked with his wife to decompress the experience. Or he stepped straight under a showerhead, still in full uniform, and let the water stream over him, the water washing away the performance he wanted to forget down the drain.

Which leads to resiliency and a drive to keep pushing, despite setbacks and bad breaks. These pitchers found a way to turn the page and not let the negativity infect their games or their outlook. How? R. A. Dickey says one way is through practice. "Practicing it and working with people that have done it and being vulnerable enough to say I don't have it figured out." And, like Dennis Eckersley in 1989, catch the ball and touch first base for the final out in the World Series and savor the moment while striking that right balance. "The high and the low," Eckersley says. "Because the highs didn't last very long, either. You're shaking hands, and it's like, oh, God, we've got to do this again. You couldn't get too carried away."

## PREPARING FOR A MOUNTAIN CLIMB

*I had played six years in a row. By that, I mean summer ball in the United States, winter ball in Venezuela, played summer ball in the United States, played winter ball in the Dominican Republic, played summer ball in the United . . . I wanted to get there [to the major leagues]. So, what I was trying to do was expose myself to as many organizations as I could.*—LaMarr Hoyt

Rarely is success overnight. It is earned through years of work and preparation. Ron Guidry spent parts of six seasons in the minor leagues before joining the Yankees to stay. Corey Kluber played parts of seven minor-league seasons prior to establishing himself as one of Cleveland's starters. LaMarr Hoyt toiled in the minors for parts of eight seasons as he worked to earn his big-league roster spot. Eight seasons after he began focusing on throwing the knuckleball, R. A. Dickey was recognized as the best pitcher in the National League. A journey led these pitchers to the pinnacle of winning the Cy Young Award, and the journeys were gradual, marathon-like climbs, not immediate sprints. True, some reached the peak sooner than others—Barry Zito was 24 years old and in his third big-league season when he won the Cy Young Award. But Zito's road to the Cy Young involved hours of practicing with his dad, absorbing insights from Randy Jones during pitching lessons, rolling up a pair of socks and pitching them in front of a mirror to see that his form was correct, performing thousands of repetitions. Not one of these pitchers simply arrived on the summit as the best pitcher in the American or National League. All devoted themselves to a climb involving hours on a field, working with their catchers, teammates, and coaches; experimenting and finding things that worked well that they made a part of their game; and practicing them. They learned to deal with pressure and failure, and after *years* of this work, they earned and achieved exceptional success, reaching that pinnacle on the mound.

# NOTES

## 1. IMPOSSIBLE REALIZED: JIM LONBORG

1. Author interview with Jim Lonborg, June 14, 2015. All quotes that follow are from the interview, unless otherwise noted.

2. www.baseball-reference.com (accessed December 19, 2020). All statistics that follow are from this resource, unless otherwise noted.

## 2. TURNING IT OVER—A NEW PITCH, NEW SUCCESS: MIKE MCCORMICK

1. Author interview with Mike McCormick, August 15, 2014. All quotes that follow are from the interview, unless otherwise noted.

2. www.baseball-reference.com (accessed December 20, 2020). All statistics that follow are from this resource, unless otherwise noted.

## 3. A DIFFERENT APPROACH: RANDY JONES

1. www.baseball-reference.com (accessed December 20, 2020). All statistics that follow are from this resource, unless otherwise noted.

2. Author interview with Randy Jones, June 4, 2017. All quotes that follow are from the interview, unless otherwise noted.

## 4. A SEASON FOR THE AGES: RON GUIDRY

1.  www.baseball-reference.com (accessed December 20, 2020). All statistics that follow are from this resource, unless otherwise noted.

2.  Author interview with Ron Guidry, November 22, 2014. All quotes that follow are from the interview, unless otherwise noted.

## 5. THE STUDENT OF PITCHING: LAMARR HOYT

1.  www.baseball-reference.com (accessed December 20, 2020). All statistics that follow are from this resource, unless otherwise noted.

2.  Author interview with LaMarr Hoyt, August 14, 2014. All quotes that follow are from the interview, unless otherwise noted.

3.  David Falkner, "Imprisoned Hoyt Can't Escape Past," *New York Times*, June 27, 1988, Sports.

4.  Falkner, "Imprisoned Hoyt Can't Escape Past."

## 6. SETTLED IN: DENNIS ECKERSLEY

1.  Author interview with Dennis Eckersley, June 15, 2015. All quotes that follow are from the interview, unless otherwise noted.

2.  www.baseball-reference.com (accessed December 20, 2020). All statistics that follow are from this resource, unless otherwise noted.

## 7. LABELS DON'T APPLY: JACK MCDOWELL

1.  www.baseball-reference.com (accessed December 20, 2020). All statistics that follow are from this resource, unless otherwise noted.

2.  Author interview with Jack McDowell, January 9, 2016. All quotes that follow are from the interview, unless otherwise noted.

## 8. FINDING 75: BARRY ZITO

1. www.baseball-reference.com (accessed December 20, 2020). All statistics that follow are from this resource, unless otherwise noted.

2. Author interview with Barry Zito, April 21, 2016. All quotes that follow are from the interview, unless otherwise noted.

## 9. CLIMB THE MOUNTAIN: R. A. DICKEY

1. Author interview with R. A. Dickey, August 23, 2019. All quotes that follow are from the interview, unless otherwise noted.

2. www.baseball-reference.com (accessed December 20, 2020). All statistics that follow are from this resource, unless otherwise noted.

3. Author interview with Josh Thole, July 24, 2019.

4. Thole interview, July 24, 2019.

5. Thole interview, July 24, 2019.

## 10. PITCHING AGGRESSIVELY: COREY KLUBER

1. Author interview with Corey Kluber, December 23, 2020. All quotes that follow are from the interview, unless otherwise noted.

2. www.baseball-reference.com (accessed December 28, 2020). All statistics that follow are from this resource, unless otherwise noted.

3. Chris Assenheimer, "The Ax-Man Cometh . . . and He Taketh Away," *Ashtabula Star Beacon*, May 5, 2014, C2.

4. Email to the author from Corey Kluber, December 23, 2020.

5. Email to the author from Corey Kluber, December 23, 2020.

6. Email to the author from Corey Kluber, December 23, 2020.

7. Email to the author from Corey Kluber, December 23, 2020.

## CONCLUSION

1. Author interview with Ron Guidry, November 22, 2014. All quotes from Mr. Guidry are from this interview unless otherwise noted.

2. www.baseball-reference.com. All statistics are from this resource unless otherwise noted.

3. Author interview with Jim Lonborg, June 14, 2015. All quotes from Dr. Lonborg are from this interview unless otherwise noted.

4. Author interview with R. A. Dickey, August 23, 2019. All quotes from Mr. Dickey are from this interview unless otherwise noted.

5. Author interview with Dennis Eckersley, June 15, 2015. All quotes from Mr. Eckersley are from this interview unless otherwise noted.

6. Author interview with Corey Kluber, December 23, 2020. All quotes from Mr. Kluber are from this interview unless otherwise noted.

7. Author interview with Jack McDowell, January 9, 2016. All quotes from Mr. McDowell are from this interview unless otherwise noted.

8. Author interview with Barry Zito, April 21, 2016. All quotes from Mr. Zito are from this interview unless otherwise noted.

9. Author interview with LaMarr Hoyt, August 14, 2014. All quotes from Mr. Hoyt are from this interview unless otherwise noted.

# BIBLIOGRAPHY

## PERSONAL COMMUNICATION

Author interview with R. A. Dickey, August 23, 2019.
Author interview with Dennis Eckersley, June 15, 2015.
Author interview with Ron Guidry, November 22, 2014.
Author interview with LaMarr Hoyt, August 14, 2014.
Author interview with Randy Jones, June 4, 2017.
Author interview with Corey Kluber, December 23, 2020.
Author interview with Jim Lonborg, June 14, 2015.
Author interview with Mike McCormick, August 15, 2014.
Author interview with Jack McDowell, January 9, 2016.
Author interview with Josh Thole, July 24, 2019.
Author interview with Barry Zito, April 21, 2016.
Email to the author from Corey Kluber, December 23, 2020.

## BOOKS, MAGAZINES, NEWSPAPERS, WEB ARTICLES

Anderson, Dave. "Sinker, Slider Bread and Butter Pitches for Jones." *Lethbridge Herald*, June 11, 1978, 32.
Antonen, Mel. "Cy Young, MVP, Manager Are Neck-and-Neck Races." *USA Today*, 2002.
Araton, Harvey. *Driving Mr. Yogi: Yogi Berra, Ron Guidry, and Baseball's Greatest Gift*. New York: Houghton Mifflin Harcourt, 2012.
Assenheimer, Chris. "The Ax-Man Cometh . . . and He Taketh Away." *Ashtabula Star Beacon*, May 5, 2014, C2.
———. "Getting Warm." *Elyria Chronicle Telegram*, April 9, 2014, C5.
———. "Matching Moneyball." *Elyria Chronicle Telegram*, September 13, 2017, B1.
———. "Meet the Indians." *Elyria Chronicle Telegram*, March 5, 2014, D3.
———. "Tribe Notes: Glad to Still Be Playing." *Elyria Chronicle Telegram*, September 23, 2014, B3.
Bisheff, Steve. "Nobody Wanted SD's Randy Jones." *Scottsdale Daily Progress*, August 20, 1976, 11.
Boeck, Greg. "A's Zito Takes Last Fall's Letdown Seriously." *USA Today*, 2002, Sports, 10c.

Brewer, Patrick. "Quantifying the Cy Young." RO Baseball. August 20, 2016. Accessed December 7, 2020. https://medium.com/ro-baseball/quantifying-the-cy-young-cdd70bbe0c08.

Broderick, Pat. "Former Padre Still Pitching . . . Food This Time." *San Diego Business Journal* 18, no. 38 (September 22, 1997): 8.

Callahan, Gerry. "Rebirth in the Bronx." *Sports Illustrated* 83, no. 7 (August 14, 1995): 44–48.

"Captain Quirk." *People* 58, no. 5 (2002): 124.

Carree, Chuck. "Column." *Wilmington Star News*, October 28, 2010.

Center, Bill. "Jones Teaching Fine Art of Sinker." *San Diego Union-Tribune*, March 13, 2013, D-1.

Chass, Murray. "With an Eye on Clemens, Guidry Recalls His Record-Setting Season of '78." *New York Times*, September 9, 2001, SP19.

Chen, Albert. "Nolan Ryan's Crusade." *Sports Illustrated* 112, no. 22 (May 24, 2010): 72–76.

———. "Rise of the Machine." *Sports Illustrated* 121, no. 19 (November 24, 2014): 54–56.

Couch, Greg. "Last Three Outs Require Mental Toughness on the Part of a Closer." *Baseball Digest* 63, no. 8 (August 2004): 54–57.

Daley, Ken. "A's Follow Winning Blueprint to the Letter." *Dallas Morning News*, 2002.

Dickey, R. A. "Moments That Make the Man." *Sports Illustrated* 116, no. 14 (April 2, 2012): 58–59.

———. *Wherever I Wind Up: My Quest for Truth, Authenticity, and the Perfect Knuckleball*. New York: Blue Rider, 2012.

Doyle, Al. "Former Cy Young Award Winner Randy Jones." *Baseball Digest* 60, no. 8 (August 2001): 64.

———. "Goose Gossage: The Game I'll Never Forget." *Baseball Digest* 64, no. 3 (May 2005): 44–46.

*Elyria Chronicle Telegram*. "Far from Perfect." July 25, 2014, C1.

———. "Skkkkkkid Over." September 17, 2014, B1.

Fagen, Herb. "Mike McCormick Recalls How It Was in 1950s and '60s." *Baseball Digest* 57, no. 7 (1998): 64.

Fagerstrom, August. "A No. 1 in Progress." *Ashtabula Star Beacon*, June 25, 2014, B2.

Falkner, David. "Imprisoned Hoyt Can't Escape Past." *New York Times*, June 27, 1988, Sports.

Fennelly, Martin. "There It Goes. . . ." *Tampa Tribune*, September 26, 2003, Sports, 1.

Fimrite, Ron. "The Good Guys against the Bad Guys." *Sports Illustrated* 47, no. 17 (October 24, 1977): 18–25.

Foltman, Bob. "White Sox See a Lot of Past in the Future." *Knight Ridder / Tribune News Service*, February 21, 2004, K4043.

Ginsburg, David. "Kluber Fires 3-Hitter as Indians Blank Orioles." *Ashtabula Star Beacon*, June 20, 2017, C1.

Goldman, Steve. "Kluber Twirls Gem." *Ashtabula Star Beacon*, July 31, 2014, C2.

Guidry, Ron, and Peter Golenbock. *Guidry*. Englewood Cliffs, NJ: Prentice Hall, 1983.

Gutierrez, Paul. "Catching up with . . ." *Sports Illustrated* 89, no. 5 (August 3, 1998): 14.

Hayes, Neil. "Different Styles Get the Same Result for A's." *Contra Costa Times*, 2005.

Herrick, Steve. "Kluber Strikes Out Season-High 14; Indians Top Blue Jays 8–1." *Lima News*, July 24, 2017, 3C.

*Hillsdale Daily News*. "Randy Jones Wins Cy Young." November 3, 1976, 4A.

Hiltbrand, David. "Strike Out the Band." *Entertainment Weekly* 311 (1996): 56.

Hoffer, Richard. "The Bandleader." *Sports Illustrated* 79, no. 5 (August 2, 1993): 30–35.

Hoffman, Benjamin. "While Mets Falter, Dickey Is Solid." *Pittsfield Berkshire Eagle*, August 14, 2012, C3.

Hollier, George. "A Louisiana Life: Ron Guidry, Louisiana Lightning." *Louisiana Life* 18, no. 2 (1998): 80.

Hoynes, Paul. "Under Pressure." *Baseball Digest* 66, no. 5 (July 2007): 50–53.

Hummel, Rick. "LaRussa Uses Bullpen However He Can to Keep Runs off Board." *St. Louis Post-Dispatch*, October 18, 2011.

———. "Players and Coaches Laud LaRussa in Ceremony." *St. Louis Post-Dispatch*, May 12, 2012.

Hunter, Bob. "Meyer Still Hot on Trail in Recruiting." *Ashtabula Star Beacon*, June 14, 2014, D7.

Hurd, Rick. "Agony or Ecstasy? It All Depends on Who Your Closer Is." *Contra Costa Times*, March 31, 2006.

———. "A's Zito Hit Early, Often by Yankees." *Contra Costa Times*, 2002.

———. "Tejada Saves Day for Zito." *Contra Costa Times*, 2002.

Jones, Chris. "He Came from Outer Space." *Esquire* 137, no. 6 (June 1, 2002): 48.

Kaplan, Jim. "Viewpoint: Possessing More Than Stats, These Three Are Worthy of Cooperstown." *Sports Illustrated* 64, no. 22 (June 2, 1986).

Keith, Larry. "Unbeaten, and All but Untouchable." *Sports Illustrated* 48, no. 27 (June 26, 1978): 20–21.

Kelly, Brad. "Boston's Carl Yastrzemski Made It All Possible." *Investor's Business Daily*, August 20, 2007, A03.

Kenney, Kirk. "Randy Jones Showed Winning Spirit in '76." *San Diego Union-Tribune*, July 8, 2016.

Kepner, Tyler. "Zito Beats Martinez to Win First Cy Young Award." *New York Times*, November 8, 2002.

Killion, Ann. "Hall of Fame Inductee Eckersley Rekindles Memories of A's Glory." *San Jose Mercury News*, 2004.

Knapp, Andrew D., and Alan S. Kornspan. "The Work of Harvey Dorfman: A Professional Baseball Mental Training Consultant." *Baseball Research Journal* (Spring 2015). https://sabr.org/journals/spring-2015-baseball-research-journal/.

Kulianin, Maria. "A's Star Zito Dogged by 'Personal' Stuff." *USA Today*, 2002, Sports, 03c.

Kurkjian, Tim. "Inside Baseball: Making It Look E-Z." *Sports Illustrated* 78, no. 20 (May 24, 1993): 58.

———. "Inside Baseball: Something's Burning." *Sports Illustrated* 80, no. 17 (May 2, 1994): 74.

———. "Short Hops." *Sports Illustrated* 79, no. 4 (July 26, 1993): 58.

LaPointe, Joe. "A's Get Better of Metrodome's Quirks." *New York Times*, October 5, 2002.

———. "One Word Describes A's: Winners." *New York Times*, September 4, 2002.

Lee, Dick. "Red Sox Pitcher Dennis Eckersley Announces His Retirement." *Providence Journal-Bulletin*, 1998.

Leggett, William. "A Wild Finale—and It's Boston!" *Sports Illustrated* 27, no. 15 (October 9, 1967): 32–37.

Leonard, Tod. "Randy Jones Gives Charity Golf Big Stakes." *San Diego Union-Tribune*, August 26, 2013.

Lewis, Ryan. "Indians' Kluber Strikes Out 11 in Complete-Game Win." *Lima News*, April 25, 2014, 4C.

*Lima News*. "Indians Kluber Strikes Out 14 Batters Again." September 22, 2014, 1B.

———. "Indians Win on Gomes' Homer." August 9, 2017, 1C.

———. "Kluber Outpitches Hernandez." July 31, 2014, C1.

Lin, Dennis. "Jones Happy to Touch Base with Padres." *San Diego Union-Tribune*, March 24, 2017, Sports, 1.

Lockwood, Wayne. "Then and Now." *San Diego Union-Tribune*, February 13, 1996, D-1.

Lonborg, Jim. "The Impossible Dream." *Boston Magazine* (July 1986): 94–97.

Malafronte, Chip. "New Haven 200: Ron Guidry Showed Flashes of Brilliance with West Haven Yankees." *New Haven Register*, July 6, 2012.

Martinez, Michael. "Guidry Shuts Out Tigers, 4–0 on 4 Hits." *New York Times*, June 23, 1985, Sports.

———. "Ron Guidry's Style Changing for Better." *New York Times*, July 22, 1985, Sports.

McCouley, Janie. "Gomes, Indians Finalize $23M, 6-Year Deal." *Sandusky Register*, April 2, 2014, B5.

McMurray, John. "Ron Guidry Recalls Glory Days with the Yankees." *Baseball Digest* 65, no. 7 (September 2006): 70–73.

Miedema, Lawrence. "A's Bank on Big Three." *San Jose Mercury News*, 2002.

———. "Zito Says He's Chased the Ghosts out of Metrodome." *San Jose Mercury News*, 2002.

Montville, Leigh. "Bitter Ending." *Sports Illustrated* 78, no. 21 (May 31, 1993): 36–41.

Morrill, Julia. "Jim Lonborg." *Sports Illustrated* 107, no. 1 (July 2, 2007): 129.

Morris, Chris. "Indie Xmas Records Slow Seasonal Shudders." *Billboard* 107, no. 50 (1995): 89.

Moses, Sam. "Yankee from Louisiana." *Sports Illustrated* 50, no. 3 (January 22, 1979): 60–72.

*New York Post*. "Dickey Sets Mets Record for Consecutive Scoreless Innings in 9–1 Win over Rays." June 13, 2012.

O'Connor, Michael. "Lonborg Makes Pitch on Slopes." *Boston Herald*, March 18, 1998, 083.

Okanes, Jonathan. "A's Fly Solo, Regain Edge against Twins." *Contra Costa Times*, 2002.

———. "Zito Continues A's Dominance." *Contra Costa Times*, 2002.

———. "Zito Puts A's Back in Familiar Territory." *Contra Costa Times*, 2002.

Parrillo, Bill. "Dennis Eckersley Did the Job and Talked Straight." *Providence Journal-Bulletin*, 1998.

Patrick, Dan. "Just My Type." *Sports Illustrated* 121, no. 3 (July 18, 2014): 23.

Pearlman, Jeff. "New Wave." *Sports Illustrated* 94, no. 2 (January 15, 2001): 44–48.

Peterson, Gary. "Cerebral Pitcher Zito Is a Student of His Craft." *Contra Costa Times*, 2002.

———. "Eck: The Man Who Rose Far above the Failure He Feared So Much." *Sporting News* 222, no. 51 (December 21, 1998): 49.

———. "Eck Opens Door for Other Closers." *Contra Costa Times*, 2004.

*Pittsfield Berkshire Eagle*. "Mets' Dickey Is Dealing." June 19, 2012, C3.

Pollard, Richard. "On the Road with the 'Freaks.'" *Sports Illustrated* 9, no. 6 (August 11, 1958): 48–50.

Pomrenke, Jacob. "Baseball Awards Date Back to Game's Earliest Days." BaseballHall.org. Accessed December 7, 2020. https://baseballhall.org/discover/baseball-awards-date-back-to-games-earliest-days.

Purdy, Mark. "Metrodome Has a Patent on Stupid Baseball Tricks." *San Jose Mercury News*, 2002.

Reynolds, Bill. "Pedro Is the 'Gentleman Jim' of 2000." *Providence Journal*, September 3, 2000.

Ridenour, Marla. "Bourn Says He's OK, But . . ." *Ashtabula Star Beacon*, March 18, 2014, B2–B3.

Rosenstein, Johnny. "Never-Say-Die-Guys." *Baseball Digest* 61, no. 11 (November 2002).

Ryan, Bob. "Saving the Eck." *Baseball Digest* 62, no. 8 (August 2003): 28–29.

Sabedra, Darren. "Barry Zito an AL Cy Young Winner." *San Jose Mercury News*, 2002.

Sandomir, Richard. "In '78 Classic Game, Things Were Simpler, and Quicker." *New York Times*, May 6, 2010, B17(L).

Schlossberg, Dan. "1967: When Carl Yastrzemski Became a Star." *Baseball Digest* 61, no. 7 (2002): 74.

*Shelby Star*. "Dickey Masters the Wild Ride." July 7, 2012, 2B.

Sherrill, Cassandra. "Ernie Shore: Field of Stars." *Winston-Salem Journal*, June 30, 2008, Sports, C1.

SI Staff. "Getting Fat with the Thin Man." *Sports Illustrated* 47, no. 12 (September 19, 1977): 76.

———. "Nobody Thinks It's the Dodgers." *Sports Illustrated* 26, no. 16 (April 17, 1967): 65–68.

Slusser, Susan. "A's Pitchers Barry Zito, Mark Mulder and Tim Hudson Talk a Good Game." *Baseball Digest* 61, no. 12 (December 2002): 48.

———. "Oakland Athletics." *The Sporting News* 225, no. 40 (October 1, 2001): 55.

———. "Oakland Athletics." *The Sporting News* 226, no. 25 (2002): 54.

Spiegel, Matt. "There Never Has Been Anyone Quite Like R. A. Dickey." *Daily Herald*, June 24, 2012, Section 2: 3.

Thompson, Rich. "Dream Comes True Again: '67 Team Enjoys an Impossible Reunion." *Boston Herald*, August 24, 2002, 043.

Tomase, John. "A True Red Sox Legend." *Boston Herald*, July 8, 2011.
*Toronto Star.* "Consecutive Saves." 2004, Sports, E09.
Verducci, Tom. "5 Days of Hardball." *Sports Illustrated* 83, no. 17 (October 16, 1995): 22–35.
*Victorville Daily Press.* "Mets' Dickey Holds Rays to One Hit." June 14, 2012, C4.
Weiner, Richard. "Young Fans Go to Planet Zito." *USA Today*, 2002, Sports, 02c.
———. "Zito Wins Mind Games." *USA Today*, 2002, Sports, 01c.
Wild, D., and E. McDonnell. "New Faces." *Rolling Stone* 608/609 (July 1991): 29.
Withers, Tom. "The Klubot Strikes Again." *Ashtabula Star Beacon*, August 4, 2017, C1.
Wittenmyer, Gordon. "Rocky Return: Oakland Takes Dome out of the Equation." *St. Paul Pioneer Press*, 2002.
"World Series No-Hit Game. Nine Innings." *Baseball Digest* 64, no. 8 (2005): 84.
Wulf, Steve. "Basebrawl." *Sports Illustrated* 79, no. 7 (August 16, 1993): 12–17.
———. "Now or Never." *Sports Illustrated* 77, no. 16 (October 19, 1992): 18–21.
———. "They're Making a Strong Pitch." *Sports Illustrated* 61, no. 15 (September 24, 1984): 26–35.
Young, Dick. "Driving Too Fast Nearly Cost Randy Jones His Life." *Long Beach Independent*, August 12, 1976, C-6.

## WEBSITES

www.baseball-reference.com
http://www.espn.com/espn/wire/_/section/mlb/id/3654105
http://m.mlb.com/glossary/pitch-types/four-seam-fastball
http://m.mlb.com/glossary/pitch-types/two-seam-fastball

# INDEX

# ABOUT THE AUTHOR

Doug Wedge has written two other baseball history books, *The Cy Young Catcher* (with Charlie O'Brien) and *Baseball in Alabama: Tales of Hardball in the Heart of Dixie*. He earned English degrees from the University of Tulsa and the University of South Carolina and a juris doctor from the University of South Carolina School of Law. He lives in Edmond, Oklahoma, with his wife, Shawn. They have four children: Jack, Annie Sloan, Sophie, and Sadie.